Understand Philosophy

For my daughter, Rebecca

Understand Philosophy

Mel Thompson

For UK order enquiries: please contact Bookpoint Ltd,
130 Milton Park, Abingdon, Oxon OX14 4SB.
Telephone: +44 (0) 1235 827720. Fax: +44 (0) 1235 400454.
Lines are open 09.00–17.00, Monday to Saturday, with a 24-hour
message answering service. Details about our titles and how to
order are available at www.teachyourself.com

For USA order enquiries: please contact McGraw-Hill
Customer Services, PO Box 545, Blacklick, OH 43004-0545, USA.
Telephone: 1-800-722-4726. Fax: 1-614-755-5645.

For Canada order enquiries: please contact McGraw-Hill
Ryerson Ltd, 300 Water St, Whitby, Ontario L1N 9B6, Canada.
Telephone: 905 430 5000. Fax: 905 430 5020.

Long renowned as the authoritative source for self-guided
learning – with more than 50 million copies sold worldwide –
the **Teach Yourself** series includes over 500 titles in the fields of
languages, crafts, hobbies, business, computing and education.

British Library Cataloguing in Publication Data: a catalogue record
for this title is available from the British Library.

Library of Congress Catalog Card Number: on file.

First published in UK 1995 by Hodder Education, part of
Hachette UK, 338 Euston Road, London NW1 3BH.

First published in US 1995 by The McGraw-Hill Companies, Inc.

This edition published 2010.

The **Teach Yourself** name is a registered trade mark of
Hodder Headline.

Copyright © 1995, 2000, 2003, 2006, 2010 Mel Thompson

Typeset by MPS Limited, A Macmillan Company.

Printed in Great Britain for Hodder Education, an Hachette UK
Company, 338 Euston Road, London NW1 3BH, by CPI Cox &
Wyman, Reading, Berkshire RG1 8EX.

The publisher has used its best endeavours to ensure that the URLs for
external websites referred to in this book are correct and active at the
time of going to press. However, the publisher and the author have no
responsibility for the websites and can make no guarantee that a site
will remain live or that the content will remain relevant, decent
or appropriate.

Hachette UK's policy is to use papers that are natural, renewable
and recyclable products and made from wood grown in sustainable
forests. The logging and manufacturing processes are expected to
conform to the environmental regulations of the country of origin.

Impression number   10 9 8 7 6 5 4 3 2 1

Year   2014 2013 2012 2011 2010

Contents

Acknowledgements

The author and publishers would like to thank the following for their permission to use copyright material in this book:

The Observer, *The Sunday Telegraph* and *The Daily Telegraph* for extracts from their respective newspapers; Chatto and Windus for the extract from Iris Murdoch's *Metaphysics as a Guide to Morals*; Penguin Books Ltd for the extract from Descartes' *Discourse on Method* and *Chambers Concise Dictionary*, 2nd edition, 2009, ISBN: 9780550103345 for it's definition of Philosophy.

Meet the author

Welcome to *Understand Philosophy*!

We're all philosophers. When there's a tough choice to be made, when faced with the facts of birth, love or death, or simply when thinking about what we want to do with our lives or what we hold dear, we all tend to ask fundamental questions and to use our reason to try to make sense of our situation. Work is no escape from it; whether it's examining the logic of a business decision, sifting the relevance of scientific data, or trying to express oneself as clearly as possible in an email, we are exercising our philosophical muscles. To me, philosophy is doing what comes naturally, but doing it in a rigorous and systematic way, not opting out when the mental going gets tough. It's a wonderful discipline for clearing the mind; a skill like no other. It's also a point of entry into the history of ideas, perusing the wisdom of the past to aid our decisions for the future.

Four decades ago, waiting to go up to university but knowing nothing of philosophy, I picked up my newly-bought copy of Bertrand Russell's *History of Western Philosophy*, sat on a river bank near my home, and started flicking through its chapters. I found that my own thoughts and questions had been aired by others before me with far greater clarity and rigor; it was an eye-opener from which I have never recovered.

Mel Thompson, 2010

Only got a minute?

According to the *Concise Chambers Dictionary*, philosophy is:

1 the search for truth and knowledge concerning the universe, human existence, perception and behaviour, pursued by means of reflection, reasoning and argument. 2 any particular system or set of beliefs established as a result of this. 3 a set of principles that serves as a basis for making judgements and decisions.

Philosophy is an activity – the attempt to understand the general principles and ideas that lie behind various aspects of life and the language we use to convey them. Political philosophy, for example, asks questions about justice and equality, about how a state should be organized.

Philosophy as a subject also involves examining 'the history of ideas' – what thinkers have said on fundamental questions over the centuries. You can examine the philosophy of a particular period – the philosophy of ancient Greece, for example, is particularly important for understanding Western thought and culture. You might look at the philosophy of the European Enlightenment, or of the twentieth century, each giving an insight into ideas that developed out of and shaped a particular period of history. But the most straightforward way of approaching philosophy is through its subject matter – the philosophy of mind, of language, of religion, of science, of politics, the theory of knowledge and so on. The latter approach is the most accessible and will therefore be the one adopted for this book.

Philosophy aims first and foremost for clarification – of thoughts, of concepts, of language. To philosophize is to think clearly and accurately. Philosophy is both an academic subject and an essential life skill.

5 Only got five minutes?

Whatever we do, we do in time. That sounds obvious and banal, but it has implications. Consider a simple action the – decision to make a cup of tea. Do I take milk in my tea, or have it black with a slice of lemon? That might suggest to you whether I am from England or continental Europe. Do I use a cup or mug? Do I take the tea back to my desk or stroll outside to take a break from work? Each of these preferences reflects my past experience – have I previously enjoyed tea with milk, or taking a break – and influences my immediate future, since as a free agent I can have input into what happens. That does not imply that I can determine the future – after all, something dramatic might intervene to stop me making my cup of tea – but my present choices reflect my intention for that future.

Everything we do is thus a process whereby our past experiences, stored in memory, shape our intentions and choices. The crucially important present moment is no more than a fleeting transition from past to future. And that applies to absolutely everything. Without the experience of time, a symphony would be reduced to a single chord. You read a book one word at a time; it only becomes reading 'a book' if you remember the words you have already read, and anticipate following the thoughts of the author and turning the page. Without a sense of what has happened in the past, it is difficult to understand or make choices in the present, and therefore impossible to shape up our ideas for the future. Someone whose memory was totally erased would be at a loss to know what to do.

So what does this have to do with philosophy?

Philosophy is both an activity and a body of knowledge. As an activity, it takes place in the present and anticipates the future.

It is the process of thinking about and reflecting on what we know, how we know it, what we approve or disapprove, what we wish to happen. In other words, it embraces the contribution of human reason, insight and intuition, injected into each fleeting moment, to shape what will happen next. It is the crucial difference between being an inanimate object (responding in a predictable way to external forces) and a living and thinking being (able to seek out its own future); it is the point at which we make a difference. Of course everyone thinks, but not everyone considers himself or herself as a philosopher – that description is reserved for those (including you, since you are reading this book) who pay conscious attention to the process of thinking and decision-making. Philosophy is not just thinking, but thinking about thinking.

But giving attention to our thinking is greatly aided by philosophy as a body of knowledge. Although circumstances are always changing, the fundamental questions that we ask remain much the same from one generation to the next, even if the answers given to them develop over time. If we give attention to philosophy as a body of knowledge, we can thus call upon the whole history of discussions about justice – each set against the particular concerns of each thinker and the times in which they were writing – to inform our present understanding.

Whenever you take an interest in a particular set of philosophical questions – about mind, or science, or religion, or ethics, or politics – you find that your reflections have implications for many other spheres of life. For convenience, we need to divide up philosophy into its different branches, but in practice they all interpenetrate. Each of them has a history, and our views on them can be informed, our perception sharpened, and our ability to take a view and argue our case assisted by paying attention to what great thinkers in the past have had to say.

10 Only got ten minutes?

In a lecture in 1854, Louis Pasteur is reported to have said 'In the fields of observation, chance favours only the prepared mind'. Why do I mention this in an introduction to philosophy? Well, it is my view that, in life as in observation, the varied situations and crises that chance throws up present both hazards and opportunities. The person that is alert and sensitive to what life is about, and who has already considered the fundamental principles of what we can know or what we should do, will hopefully be better able to grasp and use each situation to the full. It has always been appreciated that information is needed in order to make good business decisions. At one time, an advertisement for The *Financial Times* said simply 'No FT; no comment.' To me, the same thing applies to life in general: 'No philosophy; no comment.'

In general, the aims of this book are:

▶ to map out the main areas of philosophy, and to introduce some of the thinkers who have contributed to them
▶ to give an outline of some of the arguments that have been put forward
▶ to provide an overview of the fundamental concepts and ways in which philosophy has developed, so that ideas and arguments can be 'placed' in their historical context.

Reading other people's thoughts is no substitute for thinking. If this book attempts to offer 'pegs' upon which to hang a reasoned argument, it is merely a way of assisting the person who is new to philosophy to present his or her case without having to re-invent the philosophical wheel!

What we shall be examining

What can we know for certain? What constitutes sound evidence? Are there any absolute truths? These questions are dealt with under **epistemology**: the theory of knowledge. It is particularly useful to start with epistemology, because examining evidence for any claim is a useful intellectual discipline. We shall see that some philosophers (**empiricists**) start with the evidence of the senses, while others (**rationalists**) give primacy to human reason. Making sense of life requires skill and clarity in our thinking and reflecting on what we already know. However, in a confusing world, philosophy does not always offer certainties, for it often raises more questions than it answers.

We often tend to assume that science offers a straightforward and incontrovertible way of getting information about the world – and indeed, by and large that is true. But even science throws up difficult questions. Karl Popper, a major twentieth-century figure in the **Philosophy of Science**, criticized both Marx and Freud on the basis that they would not allow new evidence to falsify their theories, whereas Popper insisted that science must always remain open to have its theories overturned if new evidence contradicts them. But it is far from clear just how willing (and appropriate) it is for science to drop useful theories at the first appearance of conflicting data.

Then there is the question of **language**. Early in the twentieth-century the Logical Positivists thought that the only valid form of language was that which described the physical world, and that the meaning of a statement was seen in its method of verification. Although inspired by science, it was a very narrow approach. Originally inspired by Wittgenstein's early work, its influence waned as Wittgenstein himself changed his view, insisting that language should be understood in terms of how it is used. We are easily fooled by words. The old joke, based on an advertisement for a painkilling tablet, goes: 'Nothing works faster than …, so, next time you have a headache, take nothing!' Silly, I know, but you may be surprised just how often we are fooled into thinking that a word automatically must refer to an entity. Controversially, 'God' has suffered from that tendency, people have been enslaved in the name of 'freedom' and treated unfairly in the name of 'justice'. The scope and significance of language is hugely important.

The Philosophy of Mind not only examines the relationship between mind and body, but explores the whole range of new ideas thrown up by cognitive science. Can the mind be fully mapped by neuroscience? Can computers replicate what goes on in the human brain? Are we animated bodies, or is there something about a human being that is beyond the physical? And, if so, might we be able – at least in theory – to survive death?

The Philosophy of Religion explores what religious beliefs mean and how we should understand words like 'God'. The traditional arguments for the existence of God form the central core of this area of philosophy – not necessarily because they are convincing as arguments, but because they help to illustrate what religious belief is about.

But human beings not only seek to understand their world, they also live in it, make choices in it, and organize themselves into societies. Philosophy therefore addresses two other practical areas of life – **Ethics** and **Political philosophy**. These are of immediate importance and relevance, since everyone is involved with making moral and political decisions at some level, and an appreciation of the values and arguments that underpin ethical principles is important for transforming personal intuition about right and wrong into rational argument.

During the twentieth century, in the English-speaking world, philosophy became much concerned with issues of evidence and language. It was often assumed that philosophers were there to unpack difficult logical problems, or to clarify terms, but were most unlikely to have anything much to say about how people should live. On the continent of Europe, however, very different approaches to philosophy were being developed; these were far more directly concerned with people's experience of their own lives. Building on the work of thinkers such as Kant in the eighteenth century, or Hegel in the nineteenth, the European tradition produced **phenomenology, existentialism** and **postmodernism** – ways of that reflect thinking the complexity of human experience which have implications for art and literature as well as philosophy.

Definite answers and progress?

When studying the natural sciences, you can generally trace a progression of ideas and a gradual expansion of knowledge. By contrast, in reading philosophy, you will find that, although you can trace out the progression of ideas (who influenced whom, and so on), you will also find that progress can sometimes appear to be circular rather than linear, that the questions explored by the ancient Greeks are still very much debated today. But philosophy is always suggesting new ways of looking at questions, new ways of expressing ideas, and new views about the purpose and function of philosophy itself. But new ideas may not necessarily be an improvement on old ones.

Is not possible to live in Western Europe, or the United States, without having your language and ideas influenced by generations of thinkers. To be aware of that heritage, gives you a greater appreciation of your own culture. There is always going to be progress, because we benefit from this developing history of ideas.

For those who crave definitive answers, philosophy is likely to prove a source of constant frustration. For those who constantly ask questions, and are prepared to examine and modify their own views, it is a source of fascination and a means of sharpening the critical faculties.

Introduction

In order to enjoy philosophy, it is important to remember that it is both an activity and a body of knowledge.

As an activity, it is a matter of asking questions, challenging assumptions, re-examining traditionally held views, unpacking the meaning of words, weighing up the value of evidence and examining the logic of arguments. It cultivates an enquiring and critical mind, even if it sometimes infuriates those who want an easy intellectual life. Philosophy is also a means of clarifying your own thinking. The clearer your thought, the better able you will be to express yourself, and the more accurate your way of examining arguments and making decisions.

As a body of knowledge, it is the cumulative wisdom of great thinkers. It offers you a chance to explore fundamental questions and to see what thinkers in different periods of history have had to say about them. This in itself is valuable, because it frees you from being limited by the unquestioned assumptions of those around you. To think through issues from first principles is a natural result of having looked at the way in which philosophers have gone about their work. So this second aspect of philosophy reinforces the first.

Philosophy is a tool with which to expose nonsense, and express ideas in a way that is as unambiguous as possible. For example, philosophy makes a distinction between 'analytic' and 'synthetic' statements. An analytic statement is known to be true once the definitions of its terms are understood. 2 + 2 = 4 is just such a statement. You don't have to go out gathering sets of two items and counting them in order to verify it. You cannot return triumphant and proclaim that you have found a single case which disproves the rule – that you have two sets of two which actually add up to five! Proof, for analytic statements, does not require research or experimental testing. On the other hand, if I say that a certain person is at home, that cannot be true in the same way – it is a synthetic statement, based on evidence. To find out whether or not it is true, you have to phone or visit. The statement can easily be proved wrong, and it certainly cannot be true for all time.

But if someone says 'God exists', is that an analytic or a synthetic statement? Can you define 'God' in such a way that his existence is inevitable? If so, can any evidence be relevant for or against that claim? You might argue that:

▶ *God is everything that exists.*
▶ *Everything that exists, exists.*
▶ *Therefore God exists.*

This argument is sound, but it implies that 'God' and 'everything that exists' are interchangeable terms. This is **pantheism** (the idea that God and the world are identical) and it is quite logical, but is it what most people mean by the word 'God'? And what are its implications for the way we see 'everything that exists'? We observe that everything in the world is liable to change. There will come a time when nothing that exists now will remain. Does this mean that a pantheistic god is also constantly changing? Does it make sense for a word to stay the same, when the thing to which it refers changes? Is a school the same if its buildings are replaced, its staff move on to other posts, and its pupils leave year by year to be replaced by others? Am I the same, even though most of the cells in my body are changing, and my thoughts are constantly on the move? What is the 'I' that remains throughout my life?

In these questions we have touched on some of the central problems of philosophy:

▶ **metaphysics** – *the study of reality, of what actually exists*
▶ **epistemology** – *questions about what things we can know, and how we can know them*
▶ **philosophy of religion** – *the issues that lie behind religious ideas and language*
▶ **philosophy of mind** – *the study of the nature of the self.*

This illustrates another feature of philosophy, and a good reason to study it: you can start from any one question and find yourself drawn outwards to consider many others. Start with 'the self', and you find that matters of metaphysics or religion are drawn into your thinking. By using the skills of philosophy, you have the means of integrating your ideas, of relating them, and of testing them out within a wide range of issues.

Different styles of argument

Philosophy can be presented in different ways. Plato, for example, favoured the dialogue form. So his political philosophy in *The Republic* has a range of characters, each of who presents and argues for a particular viewpoint. Other philosophers gradually unpack the implications of their particular theory in a more linear fashion.

Some, of course, take an analytic approach, breaking down accepted ideas into their simplest indubitable elements, and then trying to start from scratch and give an account of what can be known for certain. There is also pure logic, which uses artificial languages in order to clarify and set out the logic of our ordinary language.

Much of the time, philosophy is concerned with language. Indeed, some philosophers see their whole task as linguistic. In this, it is important to distinguish between 'first order' and 'second order' language. Some examples:

First order:	'A caused B.'
Second order:	'What does it mean to say that A caused B?'
First order:	'Is it right to do this?'
Second order:	'What does it mean to say that something is "right"?'
First order:	'God does not exist.'
Second order:	'What is religious language, and how may religious assertions be verified?'

Second order language clarifies first order language. In doing so it also clarifies the thought that lies behind that language. Philosophy is mainly concerned with second order language, so it may not be able to tell you if something is right or wrong, but it will clarify the grounds upon which you can make that decision for yourself.

There was a phase in philosophy – starting early in the twentieth century – when some thinkers claimed that the sole task of philosophy was to clarify the meaning of words. They assumed that, once the linguistic problems were sorted out, all else would follow. Today that view is giving way to a broader perspective. Philosophy is indeed about language, and it is essential to understand the language you use, but it is also important to rise above language, to explore the basic ideas and concepts it expresses, and then to move on to examine features about the world that would not have come to light without that process of serious thinking and analysis.

Of course, philosophers do not always agree about how to do philosophy, or what is of value. The late A. J. Ayer, an Oxford philosopher best known for his work on 'logical positivism' (see p. 72), interviewed about his work in 1980, commented in his usual direct way on the work of various other philosophers, saying of the German existential philosopher Heidegger's idea about 'the Nothing' that it seemed to him to be 'sheer rubbish' and that people might sometimes be impressed because they like to be mystified. In Chapter 8 we shall be looking briefly at the work of Heidegger. You may feel inclined, after reading that, to agree with Ayer, or you might feel that Heidegger is describing something of greater importance than Ayer's more analytic approach. The essential thing to realize at this stage is that philosophers do not all agree on the topics about which to philosophize, the way to set about doing so, or the conclusions reached. Philosophy is not monolithic. There is no body of established and unquestioned work; it is an ongoing activity – and one which often raises more questions than it answers.

Eastern approaches

Philosophy is not limited to any one culture or continent. The philosophy introduced in this book, and taught in departments of philosophy in most universities in Europe and the United States, is Western philosophy – but that is only one part of a much larger tradition.

Eastern philosophy is generally taken to include the major religious and philosophical systems of India (the various traditions collectively known as Hinduism, along with Buddhist and Jain philosophy) and the Far East, including Confucian and Taoist thought and the later developments of Buddhism.

It is commonly said that the big difference between Eastern and Western philosophy is that the former is religious, and is concerned with salvation as much as with knowledge, whereas the latter is secular, seen by many as almost an alternative to religion. That is not entirely true. In the West, the Christian, Jewish and Muslim religions have had a profound influence on philosophical thought, and the philosophy of religion continues to be an important aspect of philosophy. In the East, although philosophy is seen as a matter of practical and spiritual importance, the process of reasoning can be examined in itself, quite apart from any religious connotations. It may also distort Eastern thought to try to draw a distinction between religion and philosophy: Buddhism, for example, sees the path to overcoming suffering in terms of understanding the fundamental truths of life. It is not a matter of religious doctrines on the one hand and secular thought on the other – that is a Western distinction that is not really relevant.

Since there is little enough scope within this book to introduce the main areas of Western thought, no attempt has been made to explore Eastern philosophy. A book on *Eastern Philosophy*, originally part of this series, is available from the same author – see 'Further Reading'.

Philosophy today – like the froth on the crest of a wave – is carried forward by the whole movement of thought that stretches back at least 2,500 years, and far longer if you include Eastern thought. What this book seeks to do (while acknowledging its limitations of coverage and depth) is to point to the reality of the wave, and the general direction of the water within it. A society without philosophy would be cut off from its own roots; it would have to start from scratch time and time again to sort out its values and its self-understanding. With philosophy, that process of sorting out is shown in its historical and logical perspectives. With philosophy, you start at an advantage, for you look at each problem with the benefit of knowing something of the accumulated wisdom of some of the best thinkers in Western culture.

Worth the hemlock?

One of the most remarkable moments in the history of Western philosophy was the death of Socrates in 399 BCE. The event is recorded by Plato, whose respect for his teacher was such that he set out most of his philosophy in the form of dialogues in which Socrates plays the central role. Charged with impiety, Socrates was condemned to death on the grounds that his questioning and teaching was corrupting the young (with whom he appears to have been popular for challenging conventional beliefs and ideas). Plato presents Socrates as declining to propose an acceptable alternative punishment, and being prepared to accept death (by drinking a cup of hemlock). For Plato, reason and the freedom of the individual to live in accordance with it, took priority over the social and political order. Socrates would not compromise his freedom to pursue the truth, even if it appeared subversive and a danger to the state. Indeed, as Plato was later to expound in *The Republic*, justice and the institutions of state should be based on reason, and rulers should be philosophers, willing and able to apply reason with disinterested objectivity.

For Socrates, the task of the philosopher was not peripheral to life, but central. To stop questioning and challenging accepted concepts was unthinkable; Socrates chose to accept death rather than leave Athens. He is presented as calm, rational and a man of absolute integrity.

Philosophy can be a frustrating discipline. Sometimes it appears dry and remote from life. Sometimes it takes the role of linguistic handmaid, clarifying the terms used by other disciplines without appearing to offer anything of substance to the sum of human knowledge. Sometimes philosophers insist on setting down their thoughts in a style that obscures rather than clarifies. From time to time, one may be tempted to ask, 'Is it worth it? Why not settle for established thoughts and values, however superficial? Why make life difficult by this constant questioning?' or, in the case of Socrates, 'Is it worth the hemlock?'

That I leave the reader to judge.

1

The theory of knowledge

In this chapter you will learn:
* *how Western philosophers have tackled the issue of knowledge and certainty*
* *how some of the best-known philosophers have described reality*
* *how to assess the role of your senses in understanding the world.*

There are two basic questions which have been asked throughout the history of philosophy and which affect the way in which many different topics are considered:

What can we know?

This question is about the basic features of existence; not the sort of information that science gives about particular things, but the questions that lie beneath all such enquiry: questions about the fundamental nature of space, time or causality; about whether concepts like 'justice' or 'love' have any external, objective reality; about the structure of the world as we experience it. In the collected works of Aristotle, such questions were dealt with after his material on physics and were therefore called **metaphysics**.

But as soon as we start considering metaphysics, yet another question arises:

How can we know it?

Is there anything of which we can be absolutely certain? Do we depend entirely on our senses, or can we discover basic truths simply by thinking? How can we justify or prove the truth of what we claim? All such questions are considered under **epistemology** – the theory of knowledge.

But when we deal with metaphysics or epistemology, we have to communicate our thoughts in some way. The medium for this is language. We ask 'What can we say?' and 'How can we say it?' The study of the nature of language, and the way in which statements can be shown to be true or false, is another constant preoccupation of philosophy.

In this chapter we shall be examining some basic issues in metaphysics and epistemology, before going on to look at scientific knowledge and the nature of language. Once you have a sound knowledge of these areas of philosophy, it will become much easier to examine the way they are applied to various topics to be considered later – God, the mind, ethics, politics and so on. You will find that the same fundamental problems occur in all areas of study.

Empiricism and rationalism

Within epistemology (the theory of knowledge) there is a fundamental issue about whether our knowledge originates in, and is therefore dependent upon, the data we receive through our senses, or whether (since we know that all such sense data is fallible) the only true certainties are those that come from our own minds – from the way in which we think and organize our experience, from the principles of reason and logic.

Two key terms:

- **Empiricism** – *all knowledge starts with the senses.*
- **Rationalism** – *all knowledge starts with the mind.*

An example of an empiricist position is that of Hume, while a rationalist one is illustrated by Descartes. Their arguments about how we can justify our claims to knowledge will be outlined later in this chapter.

However, the issue of experience and the way the mind categorizes it is far from straightforward. A very basic problem here concerns **reductionism**, and the existence of, or reality of, complex entities or general concepts.

Consider these questions:

- *How does a painting relate to the individual pigments or threads of canvas of which is it made?*
- *How does music relate to vibrations in the air?*
- *How does a person relate to the individual cells in his or her body?*
- *How does a nation relate to the citizens of which it is made up?*

A 'reductionist' approach to metaphysics takes the 'nothing but' view, for example that music is 'nothing but' vibrations in the air.

Reductionism and practical decisions ...

When, on Christmas Day, the British and German soldiers facing one another in the First World War came out of their trenches, played football together and shared cigarettes, they ceased to be merely representatives of nations and acted as individuals. Later, they returned to their trenches and continued to kill one another.

(Contd)

Which is more real – a nation or the individuals who make it up? Which should guide action? Should we act as individuals, framing political decisions on the basis of what individuals want, or should we give primacy to the 'nation' or the 'class', even if individuals have to suffer as a result? That is a matter for ethics, but we can go further and ask, 'Do nations actually exist? Is there any such thing as society, or are there just people and families?' These are fundamental, abstract questions, but they have important practical and moral consequences.

If you believe that the ultimate reality is matter – the solid external world that we experience through our senses – then you are probably going to call yourself a **materialist**. On the other hand, if you hold that the basic reality is mental – that the world of your experience is in fact the sum of all the sensations and perceptions that have registered in your mind – you may call yourself an **idealist**.

Insight

Although idealism sounds improbable, consider this: How can you tell whether, at this moment, you are dreaming or experiencing the external, physical world? If you just consider the experience you have, it's not quite as simple as common sense would suggest.

Knowledge and justification: are you certain?

Whenever I experience something, that experience involves two things:

1 *The sensations of sight, sound, taste, touch or smell, all of which seem to me to be coming from outside myself, and therefore to be giving me information about the world.*
2 *My own senses. If I am partially deaf, I may be mistaken in what I hear. If I am colour-blind I will not be able to*

distinguish certain patterns, or appreciate the subtleties of a multicoloured fabric. If I am asleep, all sorts of things may go on around me of which I am quite unaware.

Imagine that I am taken to a police station and questioned about something that is alleged to have happened in the recent past. I give my account of what I have heard or seen. If it sounds credible, or agrees with the evidence of others, I am likely to be believed. On the other hand, the police may ask, 'Are you sure about that? Is it possible that you were mistaken?' The implication is that, even if I am trying to be accurate and honest, the senses may be mistaken, and there may be two quite different ways of interpreting an experience.

When philosophers ask, 'What can be known for certain?' or 'Are the senses a reliable source of knowledge?' they are trying to sort out this element of uncertainty, so as to achieve statements that are known to be true.

Basically, as we saw above, there are two ways of approaching this problem, corresponding to the two elements in every experience.

▶ *Empiricists are those who start with the sensations of an experience, and say that all of our knowledge of the world is based on sensation.*
▶ *Rationalists are those who claim that the basis of knowledge is the set of ideas we have – the mental element that sorts out and interprets experience. Rationalists consider the mind to be primary, and the actual data of experience to be secondary.*

But before we look at these approaches in more detail, let us be clear about one category of things that we can know for certain. If I say that 2 + 2 = 4, there is no doubt about the truth of that statement. Mathematics and logic work from agreed definitions. Once those are accepted, certain results follow. They do not depend upon particular situations or experiences.

In general terms I can say that: If A = B + C, and if B and C are contained in, or implied by, the definition of A, then that statement will always be true. Understand the words and you understand its truth. Statements that are true by definition, although they are important, need not therefore detain us.

DESCARTES (1596–1650)

René Descartes placed one question centre-stage: 'Of what can I be certain?' He used the method of systematic doubt, by which he would only accept what he could see clearly and distinctly to be true. He knew that his senses could be deceived, therefore he would not trust them, nor could he always trust his own logic. He realized that he might even be dreaming what he took to be a waking reality. His approach is one that will be examined below, in the section on Scepticism. Yet the one thing Descartes could not doubt was his own existence. If he doubted, he was there to doubt; therefore he must exist. The famous phrase which expresses this is '*cogito ergo sum*' ('I think, therefore I am'). His argument is set out in his *Discourse on Method* (Section 4), 1637:

> **But then, immediately, as I strove to think of everything as false, I realized that, in the very act of thinking everything false, I was aware of myself as something real; and observing that the truth: I think, therefore I am, was so firm and so assured that the most extravagant arguments of the sceptics were incapable of shaking it, I concluded that I might have no scruple in taking it as the first principle of philosophy for which I was looking.**

Penguin Classics (trans. A. Wollaston), 1960

Descartes could doubt even his own body but, while doubting, he could not deny himself as a thinking being. All else was open to the challenge that he could be mistaken.

In many ways, Descartes' argument represents the starting point of modern philosophy (modern, that is, as compared to that of the ancient Greeks and of the medieval world), not because later thinkers have been in agreement with him but because, challenged by scepticism, they have followed his quest to find the basis of certainty and knowledge. In other words, Descartes set the theory of knowledge at the heart of the philosophical agenda.

RUSSELL (1872–1970)

Bertrand Russell's early philosophy was as hugely influential as his later writings were popular. He contributed to mathematics and logic, and introduced analytic philosophy, an approach that dominated the Anglo–American philosophical scene for half a century.

Moving on from Descartes' systematic doubt, a useful next step is to look at Russell's analysis of experience in his book *The Problems of Philosophy* (1912). He examines the table at which he sits to write. He observes that its appearance changes in different light and from different positions, and comes to the conclusion that our sense perceptions (the actual experiences of colour, shape and texture) are not the same thing as the table itself (otherwise we would have to say that the table becomes black once the light is turned out, or that it gets smaller when we walk away from it), but that we have to *infer* the table from those perceptions.

He therefore distinguishes sense data from the 'physical object' that gives rise to them.

He refers to Bishop Berkeley (see p. 19), who argued that there is nothing given in our perception of something that proves it exists even when nobody is perceiving it. In order to maintain continuity when things are not being observed, Berkeley used the idea that they were being observed by God. In other words, what we call matter (the external physical world) is only known to exist in dependence upon minds that perceive it.

Having commented on Descartes' systematic doubt, Russell points out that common sense suggests that there are ongoing objects, and that they do continue to exist when not being observed.

He gives the example of a cloth thrown over a table. Once that is done, the table cannot be observed, but it is implied by the shape of the cloth, apparently suspended in mid air. He also considers the situation where a number of people look at the same table. Unless there were to be some underlying reality, there seems to be little reason why everyone should see exactly the same thing.

He takes the idea of a cat which becomes equally hungry whether it is being observed or not. If it did not exist except when being observed, this would not make sense. Indeed, he points out that the cat's hunger is something that one cannot observe directly, and therefore (in terms of sense data) it does not exist.

All this leads him to accept the idea, given in an instinctive belief which he has no reason to reject, that there is indeed an external world which gives rise to our sense experience.

The external world: appearance and reality

As we have already seen, metaphysics examines what lies behind, or is implied by, our experience of the world. It explores general ideas such as 'goodness' or 'honesty' or 'beauty' and tries to say what role they play in our understanding of reality. Without metaphysics, the world is just a jumble of experiences without overall coherence.

Of course, it is quite possible to claim that our experience of the world is in fact a jumble of sensations without overall value, sense or direction. That is a rejection of all metaphysics. It is equally possible to seek for, and have an intuition that there should be, some overall reality and unity in the world, an understanding of which would be able to give guidance in the interpretation and valuation of individual experiences. This sense of overall coherence may be expressed in terms of belief in God, or it may not. But in either case, what is being done is metaphysics.

Of course, the debate about knowledge of external reality predates Descartes, even if he is a convenient starting point because of his radical doubt. The ancient Greeks were concerned to explore both the nature of experience and the words we use to describe it.

PRE-SOCRATIC PHILOSOPHERS

The philosophers Plato (427–347 BCE) and Aristotle (384–322 BCE) are the most important of the Greek thinkers for the subsequent history of Western philosophy, and they set much of the agenda for those who followed. Plato took his inspiration from Socrates (470–399 BCE), whose ideas are known primarily through his appearance in Plato's dialogues. But before Socrates there were a number of philosophers who were concerned with metaphysics from what would later become a 'scientific' standpoint. They sought the principles that lay behind all natural phenomena.

The pre-socratics include Thales and Anaximander from the sixth century BCE, along with the philosopher and mathematician Pythagoras, and Parmenides from the following century. Although there is no scope here to discuss them individually, they are covered in most histories of Western philosophy, and are well worth studying. Of particular interest are the views of the 'atomists', Leucippus and Demoncritus, who (anticipating Newtonian and later physics) thought of all material objects as made up of atoms, operating according to fixed laws, and who recognized that many secondary qualities (colour, etc.) were dependent upon the perceiver, rather than qualities inherent in what was perceived.

There was also a fascination with the problems of permanence and change. Heraclitus (early sixth century BCE) claimed that one could not step into the same river twice, on the grounds that the water that made it up was constantly changing. Can the river be considered a permanent entity if fresh water is always flowing down it?

Insight

This was a radical question to ask in the sixth century BCE, and one that is interestingly parallel to the metaphysics being developed by the Buddha in Northern India at about the same time.

With the benefit of 2,500 years of philosophical hindsight, the earliest thinkers may seem to have primitive ideas of cosmology and physics. What is remarkable, however, is that they should have set out to give an overall explanation of the world in the first place: to make it a 'cosmos', a unified, rationally understood world. There had been, and continued to be, myths and images by which the world could be explored and given meaning, but these pre-socratic philosophers set out to examine the nature of the world in a more systematic way, and to use their reason to formulate general principles about its fundamental structure and composition. While their contemporaries were thinking in terms of fate or the influence of the gods to explain things, they pressed ahead with what was later to develop into philosophy and science.

PLATO (427–347 BCE)

It has been said that the whole of Western philosophy is a set of footnotes to Plato, and there is a great deal of truth in that, since Plato covered a wide range of issues, and raised questions that have been debated ever since.

In *The Republic*, Plato uses an analogy to illustrate his view of human experience and his theory of knowledge. A row of prisoners sit near the back of a cave, chained so that they cannot turn to face its mouth. Behind them is a fire, in front of which are paraded various objects. The fire casts shadows of these objects on to the wall at the back of the cave, and this is all the prisoners can see. Plato thinks that this corresponds to the normal way in which things are experienced: shadows, not reality itself. But he then presents a situation in which a prisoner is freed so that he can turn round and see the fire and the objects that cast the shadows. His first impression is that the objects are not as 'real' as those images he has been accustomed to seeing. But then he is forcibly dragged up to the mouth of the cave and into the sunlight and he gradually adjusts to the light of the sun. The experience of daylight and perceiving the sun is painful, and requires considerable adjustment. Only then does it become clear to the prisoner that his former perceptions were only shadows, not reality. This, for Plato, corresponds to the journey from seeing particular things, to seeing the eternal realities of which the particulars are mere shadow-like copies.

In Plato's dialogues, Socrates debates the meaning of words as a means of getting to understand the reality to which they point. So, for example, he argues that 'Justice' is not just a word that is used to bracket certain events and situations together. Justice actually exists, as a reality over and above any of the individual things that are said to be just. Indeed, the individual things can be said to be 'just' only because we already have knowledge of 'justice' itself and can see that they share in its reality.

These general realities he calls 'Forms'. If we did not have knowledge of such Forms we would have no ability to put anything into a category. The Form of something is its essential feature, the thing that makes it what it is.

An example

If I do not know the essence of dogginess, I will not be able to tell if the animal before me is a dog or a camel. Is it possible that I am looking at a tall dog with a hump, a long neck and bad breath? Equally, could that dachshund on a lead be a humpless, short-necked, particularly squat camel?

Description requires general terms, and general terms require an understanding of essences. Only with a prior appreciation of dogginess or camelity – if that is the correct term – can I hope to distinguish between then.

The ultimate Form for Plato (and the goal of the philosophical quest) is the Form of the Good. An understanding of 'the good' enables all else to be valued; it is the equivalent of the sun that the escaped prisoner sees as he leaves the cave. So, in both the doctrine of the Forms and the analogy of the cave, Plato is describing the same process that concerns modern philosophers: the way in which we can relate our present experiences to reality itself. What Plato is saying is that our ordinary experience is no more than shadows, and that reality itself lies beyond them. We can have knowledge of the Forms, because they are known by reason, whereas the most we can have of the individual things in the world of sensation is 'true belief', since it is always provisional and changing.

But how do we come by knowledge of the Forms? In his dialogues, the protagonist (generally Socrates) challenges someone to explain the meaning of a particular concept and, by introducing examples by which to test out the explanation, refines the concept. This implies that true knowledge can be developed by the use of reason alone. But how is that possible, if all experience is of particulars? He believed that we must have had direct knowledge of the Forms in the eternal realm, before our birth into this world, but that such knowledge is then cluttered by the changing experiences of the everyday world (as we sit in our cave, watching shadows). For Plato, we do not gather knowledge, we remember it.

ARISTOTLE (384–322 BCE)

In the great legacy of Greek thought, Aristotle offers an interesting contrast to Plato. Whereas Plato explored the world of the 'Forms', known only to the intellect – a perfect world, free from the limitations of the particular things we experience – Aristotle's philosophy is based on what is known through experience. He categorized the sciences (physics, psychology and economics all come from Aristotle) and gave us many of the terms and concepts that have dominated science and philosophy (including energy, substance, essence and category).

In rejecting Plato's Forms, Aristotle nevertheless acknowledged that people needed to consider 'sorts' of things, rather than each particular thing individually (try describing something without using general terms to indicate the kind of thing it is), but he believed that the Forms (to use Plato's term) were immanent in the particulars. In other words, I may look at a variety of things that are red, and say that what they have in common is redness. The quality 'redness' is actually part of my experience of those things. But what would it mean to have absolute redness; a redness that was not a red something or other? In Aristotle's philosophy, we do not go outside the world of experience in order to know the meaning of universal concepts; we simply apply them within experience. This aimed to overcome a basic problem with Plato's Forms, illustrated by the example given below:

An example

I believe that this particular in front of me is a man.

Why? Because I have knowledge of the Form of man.

But, given that all particulars are different, how do I know that this one belongs to the category 'man'? (It could be a robot, an ape, a pre-hominoid.)

Answer: There must be a concept of 'man' over above the Form and the particular, to which I refer when I claim that the one is a particular example of the other.

But how do I know that **that** is in the right category? Only by having yet another concept of 'man' to which I can refer – and so on *ad infinitum*! (Which means that I can never know for sure that this is a man!)

This problem was recognized by Plato himself. It is generally known as the 'third-man argument'. By denying that the Form is separate from the particulars, but simply a way of describing the particular sort of thing that these particulars are, Aristotle reckoned that he had avoided this problem.

For Plato, knowledge had been limited to the world of forms, whereas the world known to the senses could yield, at best, only true belief. Eternal truths were detached from particular things. By contrast, having forms immanent within particulars, Aristotle claims that we can have true knowledge of the world of the senses.

There are many other important elements in Aristotle's metaphysics. One of them, his idea of causality, is of particular interest because it has implications both for metaphysics and also for the philosophy of religion.

Aristotle argued that everything had four causes:

1 **Material** – *the matter from which the thing is made.*
2 **Formal** – *the kind of thing that something is (i.e. the issue described in the box above).*
3 **Efficient** – *the agent that brings something about (the sense in which modern science would speak of a cause).*
4 **Final** – *the goal or purpose for which a thing is the way it is, and to which it is moving. This introduces the concept of the telos, or 'end'. If the world is rational, everything has its part to play, its purpose.*

This had a considerable impact on the later philosophy of religion (as we shall see in Chapter 5) and also on the 'natural law' approach to ethics (see Chapter 6). It is also important because it acknowledges that the reality of a particular thing is not just a matter of its present substance and form, but is related to agents in the past that have produced it and goals in the future to which it moves – both of which are part of its reality.

Insight
When science asks 'Why?' it looks for an 'efficient' cause or causes. When a religious or moral thinker asks 'Why?' he or she is asking about the 'final' cause or purpose.

In some way, every metaphysical question has to take account of the fact that there are individual things which need to be known and related to one another, but also (and implied every time we use language) that there are universals, general concepts, a sense of the whole. Which of these should take priority?

This dilemma is illustrated by two major metaphysical systems, those of Spinoza and Leibniz. Both are examples of rationalism (that one can come to a knowledge of reality by means of pure reason, as opposed to empiricism, which based knowledge on the data of experience), and both follow the tradition established by Descartes of trying to move from first principles to construct an overall view of the world.

SPINOZA (1632–77)

Baruch Spinoza was born to Jewish parents in Amsterdam, and was brought up in the Orthodox Jewish community, but expelled from it at the age of 24 for his heterodox views. Thereafter he earned his living grinding lenses, which allowed him freedom to develop his ideas and to write. He was later offered a professorship, but declined it in order to maintain his freedom to explore philosophy in his own way.

For Spinoza (and for Leibniz) the reality of the world, as known to reason, is very different from the appearance of the world as it is known to us through experience. Spinoza, a radical Jewish thinker, argued that God was the only absolute substance. His argument may be summarized as:

- *If God is infinite, he must co-exist with everything.*
- *God must therefore be the only thing whose explanation lies within itself (all limited things can be caused by something external – but God can't, because there is nothing external to God).*
- *God is therefore the whole of the natural order.*
- *Although individual things may appear to be separate, they are, in reality, parts of a larger whole, which is God.*
- *The one true thing is the world as a whole.*

Insight

Spinoza considered that everything therefore only had its reality as part of a greater whole, and that the mental and the material were two different aspects of the same fundamental reality. In his quest for the real, his conclusions were therefore exactly the opposite of those of Descartes.

LEIBNIZ (1646–1716)

Born in Leipzig, the son of a professor of moral philosophy, Gottfried Wilhelm Leibniz was a brilliant philosopher, mathematician (he developed calculus independently of Newton) and logician.

Leibniz takes a view about particulars and wholes which is exactly the opposite of Spinoza. For Leibniz (following Descartes) the world is divided between mental things and physical or material things, and the essential difference between them is that physical things exist in space, but mental things do not. Now Leibniz saw that any material thing can be divided into its constituent parts, and these can be sub-divided again and again. Ultimately, the world must therefore consist of an infinite number of things, which cannot be divided any more. But if they are indivisible, they cannot occupy space (if they did, they could be divided), so they cannot be physical. Therefore (since things are either physical or mental) they must be mental in nature. He called them monads.

His argument might be expressed thus:

▶ *Every complex material thing can be divided into its constituent parts.*
▶ *These parts can be sub-divided again and again.*
▶ *Anything which has extension in space can be divided.*
▶ *Ultimately you arrive at an infinite number of monads, which occupy no space at all. They cannot be physical (otherwise they would be in space, and capable of being further divided), so they must be mental.*

Note

In modern usage, 'mental' is taken to refer to the process of human thought, and as such it is difficult to see how Leibniz's monads can be so described. Given that, following Descartes, everything was designated either material or mental, Leibniz did not have much of a choice. Perhaps, in modern terms, it might be better to describe his monads as having a quality of pure energy or pure activity. This would bring his concept much closer to that of modern physics, where ultimately all matter is comprised of energy.

How do these monads come together to form complex entities? Leibniz took the view that the monads – since they were not physical – could not influence one another directly. Rather, the world was arranged with a pre-established harmony, so that all the separate monads, each following its own course, actually managed to combine to give rise to the world we know, with its complex bodies.

In other words

▶ *Which is more real – the whole or the parts of which the whole is comprised?*
▶ *Are there such things as justice and beauty (or any universal idea) or are there just individual things that we choose to describe as just or beautiful?*
▶ *How do you get beyond the things that appear to the senses? Is there a reality that lies beneath them and, if so, can we ever get to understand it?*

These are some of the basic questions for metaphysics, raised by the philosophers we have considered so far in this chapter.

STARTING WITH EXPERIENCE

In the quest for knowledge, there are two contrasting approaches: one (rationalism) starts with the mind; the other (empiricism) starts with experience. The essential thing to grasp as we look at empiricism is that sense data (which make up the content of our experience) are not simply 'things' out there in the world. They depend upon our own faculties – the way in which we experience as well as what we experience.

The rationalism/empiricism debate can be seen by contrasting Descartes' views (as briefly outlined above) with those of John Locke, George Berkeley and David Hume, who are key figures in the development of empiricism.

LOCKE (1632–1704)

John Locke is known both for his empiricism, analysing sense experience and the way in which we learn, and also for his political philosophy. In his *Essay Concerning Human Understanding* (1689), he was on the same quest as Descartes: the desire to know what the mind can comprehend and what it cannot. But his conclusions were radically different. He claimed that there are no such things as innate ideas, and that all that we know comes to us from experience, and from reflecting upon experience.

Locke held that there are primary qualities (solidity, extension, motion, number) and secondary qualities (colour, sound, taste, etc.). The former inhere in bodies (i.e. they are independent of our perceiving them); the latter depend upon the act of perception (i.e. being able to see, hear, etc.).

He also held that we can genuinely know of the existence of bodies through our senses. The sense data we receive cannot be subjective, because we do not control them. (This is similar to the position outlined by Russell as he looks at his table – because others see it as well as he, he concludes that the table itself cannot depend upon his own sensation, even if the actual data he receives does so.)

Locke was certainly influenced by Descartes. He had to accept that substance itself was unknowable, for he could know nothing directly, only through his senses. In this he anticipated to some extent the more general conclusions of Kant (see p. 23), who later made the radical distinction between things as they are in themselves (noumena) and things as we perceive them (phenomena).

BERKELEY (1685–1753)

Bishop George Berkeley was a fascinating character. He wrote his philosophy while in his twenties, later became a Bishop, and took an interest in higher education in the American Colonies (where he lived for some time), leaving his library of books to Yale University.

Berkeley argued for '**idealism**', which is the theory that everything that exists is mental. This sounds an unlikely view to hold about the world, but it follows from the way in which we perceive things. An idealist might argue as follows:

▶ *All we actually know of the world are sensations (colour, sound, taste, touch, the relative positions of things that we perceive). We cannot know the world by any other means. For us, these sensations are what we mean by 'the world'.*
▶ *All these sensations are 'ideas': they are mental phenomena. (The colour red does not exist independent of the mind perceiving something of that colour.)*
▶ *Things are therefore collections of these ideas; they exist by being perceived.*

The obvious problem for Berkeley was showing how something can exist while not being perceived.

A silly example

I am aware of a tree in front of me. I see the trunk, branches and leaves with their different colours. I may reach forward and touch the bark. The tree, for me, is the collection of all these sensations. In order

(Contd)

to test out idealism, I shut my eyes, put my hands by my side, and attempt to cut off all sensations of the tree. Convinced that the tree no longer exists, I step forward. The tree immediately reappears in the form of an acute pain in the nose and forehead!

But what does it mean to say that the tree exists in the moment between shutting my eyes and hitting the trunk?

It is possible to say that an object continues to exist if it is being perceived by someone else; but what if nobody perceives it? Berkeley's answer to this is that the tree continues to exist only because it is being perceived by God.

In thinking about Berkeley's theory, it is worth reflecting on where sensations are located. Because they take place as a result of brain and sensory activity, Berkeley says that they are mental – in effect, that they are taking place 'in' the mind. But just because a sensation varies with different conditions, as colours change with different lighting, does that imply that the whole of what we mean by colour is subjective?

Berkeley also held that there are no abstract general ideas. If you think of a triangle, you are thinking of a particular triangle. It shares its qualities with other triangles, but there is no concept of triangle that does not spring from some particular triangle. What we think of as a 'universal' is just a set of qualities abstracted from particulars.

Insight

Few things are new in philosophy. The discussion given above can be traced back to the different views of Plato and Aristotle. If you believe that universals are 'real' then you are likely to be called a 'realist' and will tend to agree with Plato, but if you think that universals are only the 'names' we give to groups of individuals, you are a 'nominalist' and will tend to agree with Aristotle.

HUME (1711–76)

David Hume was a popular and radical philosopher and man of letters who lived in Edinburgh and contributed to the eighteenth-century Scottish Enlightenment. In his day, he was better known – and more widely read – as a historian than as a philosopher, having produced a six-volume history of England. In taking an empiricist approach – that all knowledge is derived from sense experience – Hume made the important distinction (which we have already discussed) between what we have called 'analytic' and 'synthetic' statements. In other words, between:

▶ *those statements that show the relationship between ideas. These are known to be true a priori (before experience) because their denial involved contradiction, e.g. the propositions of maths and logic. They offer certainty, but not information about the world.*

and

▶ *those that describe matters of fact. These can only be known a posteriori (after experience). They are not certain, but depend on empirical evidence.*

This leads to what is known as Hume's Fork. In this, you may ask of a statement:

▶ *Does it contain matters of fact? If so, relate them to experience.*
▶ *Does it give the relationships between ideas?*
▶ *If neither, then it is meaningless.*

Insight
The problem with this is that it suggests that moral, religious or value statements are meaningless, since they do not simply depend on facts nor on pure logic. We shall examine this later, because it was a view taken up by the Logical Positivists in the twentieth century, but notice how this strictly empiricist approach limits the function of language to one of picturing the world as it is, rather than shaping it as we wish it to be.

Hume's argument concerning evidence runs like this:

- ▶ *I see something happen several times.*
- ▶ *I therefore expect it to happen again.*
- ▶ *I get into the mental habit of expecting it to happen.*
- ▶ *I may be tempted to project this mental habit out on to the external world in the form of a 'law' of physics.*

So, for example, 'A causes B' could be taken to mean 'B has always been seen to follow A'.

It might be tempting to say 'Therefore B will always follow A', but this would imply that nature is uniform, and you can never have enough evidence for such an absolute statement.

To the statement 'Every event must have a cause' Hume would say:

- ▶ *it can't be justified by logic, since its denial does not involve self-contradiction*
- ▶ *it can't be proved from experience, because we cannot witness every event.*

What, then, are we to do? Hume says that we can accept the idea of causality because it is a habit of the imagination, based on past observation. This may seem obvious, but an important distinction has been made between claiming that something *must be* the case, and saying that, in practice, we have always *found it to be* the case.

In section 10 of *An Enquiry Concerning Human Understanding* (1758), where Hume is considering miracles, he sets out his position about evidence:

A wise man ... proportions his belief to the evidence. In such conclusions as are founded on an infallible experience, he expects the event with the last degree of assurance, and regards his past experience as a full proof of the future existence of that event. In other cases, he proceeds with more caution: He weighs the opposite experiments: He considers which side is supported by the greater number of experiments: to that side he inclines, with doubt and hesitation; and when at last he fixes his judgement, the evidence exceeds not what we properly call probability.

Hume's approach is also valuable in assessing the question of whether or not the external world exists, and whether we could prove it to exist. He says that it cannot be proved, but gives two features of experience which lead to the idea being accepted – constancy and coherence. I see that objects remain in the same place over a period of time, and I assume that they remain there even when not observed. Also, I may see someone at different times in different places, and I infer from this that they are moving about. In other words, the assumption that the world is predictable enables me to fill in the gaps of my own experience. Once again, however, the key thing to remember is that this is not something that can be proved.

KANT (1724–1804)

Immanuel Kant is one of the most influential figures in the development of Western philosophy. His entire life was spent in Königsberg in East Prussia, where he was a professor at the university. This in itself was remarkable since, prior to the twentieth century, most philosophers were not professional academics.

In many ways, Kant's philosophy can be seen as an attempt to take seriously the claims of the Empiricists (e.g. Hume) that everything depends upon experience and is open to doubt, but to do so in the context of Newtonian physics and the rise of science. Science seeks to formulate laws which predict with certainty, and causality is an essential feature of Newtonian science. We just *know* that everything will be found to have a cause, even before we experience it. So how can you reconcile an empiricist view of knowledge with common sense and the findings of science?

Kant sought to achieve this through what he called his 'Copernican Revolution'. Just as Copernicus totally changed our perception of the world by showing that the Earth revolved round the Sun and not vice versa, so Kant argued that the world of our experience is shaped by our own means of perceiving and understanding it, making the important distinction between what we perceive with our senses (which he called **phenomena**) and the world of things as they are in themselves (which he called **noumena**).

Kant argued that certain features of experience, including space, time and causality, were not in themselves features of the external world, but were imposed by the mind on experience. This was a revolutionary way of looking at the theory of knowledge and at metaphysics. Take the example of time. When I see a sequence of things, I say that time is passing and that one thing follows another. But where is that time? Is it something that exists 'out there' to be seen? Is time there to be discovered? Kant argued that time was one of the ways in which the mind organizes its experiences; it is part of our mental apparatus.

▶ *'But what happened before the "Big Bang"?' is an example of the mind trying to impose the category of time on something to which scientists try to tell us it cannot be applied. However much I accept the idea of space and time coming from that 'singularity', my mind rebels and demands yet more space and time before and beyond it. I am given a description of the universe, and ask 'But what lies outside it?' If I am told that nothing lies outside it, I become confused, for my mind automatically tries to imagine an expanse of nothingness stretching outward from what is known.*

The same is true for causality. We assume that everything has a cause. Even when we have no evidence of a cause, we believe that one will be found eventually – because that is the way the world works. Kant would say that it is the way the mind works. We impose the idea of causality on our experience.

This was his way of reconciling these two important elements in the consciousness of the eighteenth century, and it has many implications for later thought.

'**Realism**' is a term that is frequently used in discussions of appearance and reality. It stands for the view that science is able to give us a true representation of the world 'out there', including entities that are unobservable. There are different forms of realism: 'naïve realism' is generally used for the view that what we perceive is what is actually there; 'representative realism' takes one step back from this, but says that we can form correct representations of what exists. This is particularly important for the philosophy of science, which we shall examine in the next chapter.

Intuitive knowledge

Intuitive knowledge creates particular problems for those who base their knowledge of the world on sense experience. For example, I may feel, listening to a piece of music or looking at a painting, that it 'says something' about life – something that is far beyond any analysis of the particular notes being played or the particles of pigment on canvas. I may feel caught up in an experience of a level of reality of which I am intuitively convinced, but which I subsequently fail to articulate precisely.

A little alcoholic drink can have the same effect – an opening up of intuitive faculties, and a conviction that suddenly the whole world makes sense, that there is something of universal importance that one wants to say. But somehow, once sober again, it is difficult to put into words.

A. J. Ayer, interviewed in *The Observer* in 1980, was asked whether, when listening to music, there might be something other than what is scientifically verifiable; whether, for example, there could be a sense of ecstasy, and of something that was not fully explained. He replied:

> *'I don't particularly want to reduce aesthetic experiences to anything expressible in purely physical terms, but I don't think it's more mysterious than any other statement you might make about yourself. Clearly there is a problem about communicating feelings of any kind, since one has to take the other person's word for it. I can't, as it were, get inside your head and measure your ecstasy, but the statement that you feel ecstatic doesn't seem to me to create any particular problem. I know roughly what kind of feeling you're describing, what causes it, how it leads you to behave, when you are susceptible to it, how it fits in with the general pattern of your behaviour. Is the fact that you feel ecstatic more mysterious than that you feel bored, or any other sort of feeling?'*
>
> *The Observer*, 24 February 1980, p. 35

Notice what is really happening in Ayer's answer. The questioner implied that there could be an intuition, in moments of ecstasy, which seemed to give awareness of something beyond scientific analysis. What Ayer does is to reduce it to the actual feeling – ecstasy – along with other feelings, like boredom. Having done that, the whole of the experience is one of understanding the internal workings of another person and his or her feelings. But what was being asked about was not ecstasy as 'feeling' but ecstasy as 'knowledge' – and it is just this that Ayer does not accept.

Note

Many things are intuited before they are understood – whether it be Einstein's intuition of relativity, or a mathematician who described a particular mathematical argument as 'elegant'. There may be a sense that something is right, even if, without further examination, it cannot be shown to be so.

Insight

It seems to me that a suitable analogy for the process of reducing intuitive knowledge to empirical evidence is that of taking a car engine to pieces in order to discover the joy of motoring. It's fine as an academic exercise, but you can't drive the car while it's in a dismantled state, and it certainly does not get you any closer to the experience of the road! Intuition is the driving force of creative thinking; analysis and assessment come later.

Scepticism

The term 'sceptic' is generally used of a person who claims that we cannot know anything for certain, and that one view is likely to be as valid as any other. People tend to be sceptical about particular things – the validity of scientific claims, for example, or politics or morals.

It may be helpful, however, to make a distinction between scepticism as a conclusion and sceptical questioning as a process. Philosophers need to question and challenge all claims to knowledge, so – as a process – being sceptical about a claim is both valid and important for philosophy. However, there are some sceptical conclusions – for example, that the world as we know it may not exist at all, but may all be a dream – that are an interesting challenge, because common sense tells you that they are wrong, but the arguments for them may be difficult to refute.

Descartes was particularly concerned about scepticism, and wanted to counter it by finding something that he could not doubt. In order to achieve this, he set about using the very process that proved so threatening: sceptical doubt. This is how he sets about his task in Section 4 of his *Discourse on Method* (1637):

> *I had noticed long ago ... that in matters of morality and custom, it is often necessary to follow opinions one knows to be highly*

doubtful, just as if there were no doubts attaching to them at all. Now, however, that I intended to make the search for truth my only business, I thought it necessary to do exactly the opposite, and to regard as absolutely false anything which gave rise in my mind to the slightest doubt, with the object of finding out, once this had been done, whether anything remained which I could take as indubitable.

(translation: A. Wollaston, Penguin Classics, 1960)

Therefore, recognizing that his senses sometimes deceived him, he decided to assume that they always did so. Equally, he recognized that people could be mistaken in their reasoning, so logic and mathematics could not be accepted as indubitable. He even went on to assume that the world as he encountered it was perhaps no more than a dream:

Finally, in view of the fact that those very same ideas, which come to us when we are awake, can also come when we are asleep without one of them then being true, I resolved to pretend that everything that had ever entered my mind was as false as the figments of my dreams.

Having done this, he reaches the conclusion that the only thing he cannot doubt is that he exists as a thinking being, for the very act of doubting requires him to think. Hence his famous starting point for knowledge 'I think, therefore I am'.

Having reached that point, he then tries to build up an account of what he can actually know – and it is this process, along with his one point of certainty, that the true sceptic will not accept. Scepticism is significant within the philosophy of religion (where the ability to know religious truths by way of reason alone may be challenged by those who emphasize the role of faith) and the philosophy of science (where realism is challenged by a variety of equally valid ways of describing the same phenomenon), as well as within discussions of the theory of knowledge.

The proof of the pudding ...

When examining matters of epistemology, you may be tempted to take a common-sense view: that a theory would seem to be right because it is the generally accepted and practical way of looking at things. We may be justified in accepting a theory if it is useful and solves problems. There is a tradition of philosophy that follows this line of reasoning: **pragmatism**. It was developed in America and is associated in particular with C. S. Peirce (1839–1914), William James (1842–1910) and John Dewey (1859–1952). In the simplest of terms, pragmatism says:

▶ *We act; we are not just spectators. The 'facts' about the world are shaped by our concerns, and what we hope to do.*
▶ *Beliefs should accord with known facts. But what should you do if the evidence is balanced between two theories?*
▶ *The answer – according to the pragmatists – is to accept the theory which gives the richer consequences; in other words, the one which will be of the greater practical use.*

Dewey emphasized the fact that we are not detached observers, but that we need to survive in the world, and that *thinking is a problem-solving activity* related to that need. Science is a dynamic process of gaining knowledge, enabling us to get some mastery over our environment. Knowledge is therefore of practical importance in our lives, not simply something about which we might speculate.

A basic test to be applied to all statements is that of *coherence*. At any one time, we have a number of ways of seeing the world and working within it. A new theory, if it is to be accepted, needs to be compatible with existing accepted theories. Of course, this cannot be an absolute criterion of truth, or truth would be decided by committee and science would make no progress. Nevertheless, it is an important factor to be taken into account. This issue of testing out new views will be considered again when we examine the philosophy of science.

Some conclusions

Knowing is a creative activity, and always involves an element of interpretation. We know nothing with absolute certainty, except those things that are true by definition. On the other hand – as we saw Russell doing as he contemplated his desk – we can gradually build up a degree of reasonable certainty.

Early in this chapter we looked at Descartes and his systematic doubt – his determination to set aside all previously held opinions and accept only what he could see clearly and distinctly to be true. In practice, however, we need to get beyond a position of total scepticism. Descartes himself saw no reason to believe that the created order should deceive us – and therefore he could accept as true what he perceived clearly to be so. Russell (in *The Problem of Philosophy*) came to accept the reality of the external object (his table) on the grounds that it was seen by a number of different people at the same time, and that its shared experience was a valid basis for asserting the objectivity of the table.

Perhaps, after all, there is scope for common sense in philosophy!

In terms of epistemology, we saw that the American pragmatist tradition looked to accept those ideas and theories that were most productive, most useful, recognizing that human beings do not simply contemplate the world but are – at least on a temporary basis – part of it, and engaged in the business of living.

A similar test might be applied to metaphysics in general. Consider the practical and emotional implications of Plato's theory of the

Forms. It is possible for a Platonic approach to lead to a view that the present world, as encountered by the senses, is inferior, partial and lacking in inherent value. The philosopher is constantly looking beyond what is present, out to another, ideal world. Justice, love, beauty, truth – if these are encountered at all in the present world they are but pale reflections of their abstract, ideal counterparts.

The religious implications of this (and indeed, the influence of Plato on the development of the Christian religion) is considerable. Reality, from this perspective, is located outside the present known world, not within it. By contrast, a materialist may insist that everything is of value in itself and needs no external or ultimate justification.

Insight

Even if we are not conscious of them, the issues considered under epistemology and metaphysics are still relevant to our ordinary concerns about the world; they shape how we see things and how we value them.

A personal postscript

A fundamental problem within Western philosophy has been caused by the view that 'self' and 'world' are separate things, with the one trying to find out if the other is actually there – a view propounded by Descartes. In my opinion, this is mistaken. In reality, what we call 'self' is a temporary and changing part of what we call 'world'. There are not two separate realities, only one, and we are part of it.

Equally, experience is not an object (sense data do not exist); it is the term we use for the relationship that all sentient beings have with the rest of the world. It is both physical and mental; it is sharing not gathering; it is plastic not fixed. If we fail to experience

(Contd)

the world around us we are likely to die, for we are part of it and depend upon the rest of it for our very existence.

In terms of metaphysics and epistemology, philosophies can be rated according to how well they account for the fundamental unity and interconnected nature of everything. On this basis, Plato, Descartes and Kant do rather badly; their worlds are fundamentally dualist. Reality, for them, is always beyond what we experience. Aristotle, Spinoza and the Pragmatists do better. For them, there is one world, and we need to engage with it and make sense of it.

10 THINGS TO REMEMBER

1 *Rationalism claims that knowledge starts with the mind; empiricism that it starts with information given by the senses.*

2 *Descartes could doubt everything except that he was thinking.*

3 *Locke distinguished between primary and secondary qualities.*

4 *For Berkeley, to be is to be perceived.*

5 *Hume argued that belief should be proportional to evidence.*

6 *Kant argued that our minds shape how we experience the world.*

7 *It is always difficult to articulate what intuition reveals.*

8 *Scepticism has a positive role in challenging claims to knowledge.*

9 *Pragmatism sees thought as a problem-solving activity.*

10 *All knowledge involves an element of interpretation.*

2

The philosophy of science

In this chapter you will learn:
- *the historical development of science in relation to philosophy*
- *the way in which scientific theories are derived from observations and experiments*
- *the issues about how science makes progress.*

The philosophy of science examines the methods used by science, the ways in which hypotheses and laws are formulated from evidence, and the grounds on which scientific claims about the world may be justified.

Philosophy and science are not in principle opposed to one another, but are in many ways parallel operations, for both seek to understand the nature of the world and its structures. Whereas the individual sciences do so by gathering data from within their particular spheres and formulating general theories for understanding them, philosophy tends to concern itself with the process of formulating those theories, and establishing how they relate together to form an overall view. We saw in Chapter 1 that metaphysics is the task of understanding the basic structures of reality that lie behind all the findings of individual sciences.

A major part of all philosophy is the process of analyzing the language people use and the criteria of truth that they accept.

Therefore, while the individual sciences use 'first order language' (speaking directly about physical, chemical or biological observations), philosophy uses 'second order language' (examining what it means to speak about those things) and examines whether the claims that are made are logically justified by the evidence on which they appear to be based.

Insight

Today, scientists specialize because it is quite impossible for anyone to have detailed knowledge of the current state of research in all the various branches of science. It is even more difficult for a philosopher to get a view of the workings of science 'as a whole'. Hence the main task of philosophy is to examine the logic of particular scientific claims, and to probe the limits of what can be said.

Scientists, mathematicians and philosophers work in separate disciplines, even if they are interested in and may benefit from the work of the others, but it was not always so. Physics was originally known as 'natural philosophy', and some of the greatest names in philosophy were also involved with mathematics and science. Aristotle examined and codified the various sciences within his overall scheme of philosophy. Descartes, Leibniz, Pascal and Russell were all mathematicians as well as philosophers. Indeed, Russell and Whitehead argued in *Principia Mathematica* (1910–13) that mathematics was a development of deductive logic – see p. 85. Bacon, Locke and others were influenced by the rise of modern scientific method, and were concerned to give it a sound philosophical basis. Kant wrote *A General Natural History and Theory of the Heavens* in 1755 in which he explored the possible origin of the solar system.

Some philosophical movements (e.g. Logical positivism, in the early years of the twentieth century – see p. 71) were influenced by science and the scientific method of establishing evidence. Many of the philosophers that we considered in the chapter on the theory of knowledge can therefore reappear in considering science, largely because scientific knowledge and its methods are such an important part of our general appreciation of what we know and how we know it.

In order to put these things into an historical perspective, however, we shall take a brief look at some of the philosophers who commented on, or were influenced by, science.

An historical overview

Within Western thought there have been two major shifts in the view of the world, and these have had an important influence on the way in which philosophy and science have related to one another. We may therefore divide Western philosophy of science into three general periods: early Greek and Mediaeval thought; the Newtonian world-view; and twentieth-century developments (although recognizing that such division represents a simplification of a more complex process of change).

EARLY GREEK AND MEDIAEVAL THOUGHT

In 529 CE the Emperor Justinian banned the teaching of philosophy in order to further the interests of Christianity. Plato had already had a considerable influence upon the development of Christian doctrines, and elements of his thought – particularly the contrast between the ideal world of the forms and the limited world of everyday experience – continued within theology. The works of Aristotle were preserved first in Byzantium and then by the Arabs, being rediscovered in the thirteenth century, when the first translations were made from Arabic into Latin.

In the thirteenth century, with thinkers like Thomas Aquinas (1225–74), Duns Scotus (1266–1308) and William of Ockham (c. 1285–1349), Greek thought began to be explored again in a systematic way. From that time, philosophy is very much a development of, or reaction to, the work of the Greeks.

It is only with Descartes (see p. 6) that it starts again from first principles, and this coincided with the development of 'modern science'.

Aristotle set out the different branches of science, and divided up living things into their various species and genera – a process of classification which became a major feature of science. He had a theory of knowledge based on sensations which depended on repetition:

sensations repeat themselves	→	**leading to perception**
perceptions repeat themselves	→	**leading to experience**
experiences repeat themselves	→	**leading to knowledge**

Thus, for Aristotle, knowledge develops out of our structured and repeated perception of evidence that comes to us from our senses – an important feature of the philosophy of science.

He also established ideas of space, time and causality, including the idea of the Prime Mover (which became the basis of the cosmological argument for the existence of God – see p. 161. He set out the four 'causes' (see p. 14), thus distinguishing between matter, the form it took on, the agent of change and the final purpose or goal for which it was designed. He considered a thing's power to be its potential. Everything had a potential and a resting place: fire rises up naturally, whereas heavy objects fall. Changes, for Aristotle, are not related to general forces like gravity (which belong to the later Newtonian scheme), but to the fact that individual things, by their very nature, have a goal.

Let us look at a few examples of the influence of Plato and Aristotle:

For Plato, the unseen 'Forms' were more real than the individual things that could be known through the senses. This way of thinking (backed by religion) suggested that human reason and its concepts of perfection were paramount, and that observation and experience were secondary.

Cosmology and astronomy give examples of this trend: Copernicus (1473–1543) and later Galileo (1564–1642) were to offer a view of the universe in which the Earth revolved around the Sun, rather than vice versa. Their view was opposed by those whose idea of the universe came from Ptolemy and in which the Earth was surrounded by glassy spheres – perfect shapes, conveying the Sun, Moon, planets in perfect circular motion. Their work was challenged (and Galileo condemned) not because their observations were found to be at fault, but because they had trusted their observations, rather than deciding beforehand what should be the case. Kepler (1571–1630) concluded that the orbit of Mars was elliptical, whereas all heavenly motion was thought to be perfect, and therefore circular.

These astronomers were struggling against a background of religious authority which gave Greek notions of perfection priority over observations and experimental evidence. In other words, the earlier mediaeval system of thought was deductive (it deduced what should be observed to happen from its pre-conceived ideas), in contrast to the later inductive method of developing a theory from observations.

Along with the tendency to look for theory and perfection rather than accept the results of observation, there was another, stemming from Aristotle. Following his idea of the final cause, everything was thought to be designed for a particular purpose. If something falls to the ground, it seeks its natural purpose and place in doing so. So, in a religious context, it was possible to say that something happened because it was God's will for it, or because it was designed for that purpose.

Insight

From this perspective, there was less interest in looking for a scientific principle or law to explain events in terms of 'efficient' causation.

The rise of modern science would not have been possible without the renewed sense of the value of human reason and the ability to challenge established ideas and religious dogma, which developed as a result of the Renaissance and the Reformation. But what was equally influential was the way in which information was gathered and sorted, and theories formed on the basis of it. Central to this process was the method of induction, and this was set out very clearly (and in a way that continues to be relevant) by Francis Bacon.

Bacon (1561–1626) rejected Aristotle's idea of final causes, and insisted that knowledge should be based on a process of induction, which, as we shall see later, is the systematic method of coming to general conclusions on the basis of evidence about individual instances that have been observed. He warned about 'idols' that tend to lead a person astray:

▶ *the desire to accept that which confirms what we already believe*
▶ *distortions resulting from our habitual ways of thinking*
▶ *muddles that come through our use of language (e.g. using the same word for different things, and then assuming that they must be one and the same)*
▶ *believing things out of allegiance to a particular school of thought.*

Bacon also pointed out that, in gathering evidence, one should not just look for examples that confirm a particular theory, but one should actively seek out and accept the force of contrary examples. After centuries of using evidence to confirm what was already known by dogma or reason, this was quite revolutionary.

The general view of the world which came about as a result of the rise of science is usually linked with the name of Isaac Newton (1642–1727). In the Newtonian world-view, observation and experiment yield knowledge of the laws which govern the world.

In it, space and time were fixed, forming a framework within which everything takes place. Objects were seen to move and be moved through the operation of physical laws of motion, so that everything was seen as a machine, the workings of which could become known through careful observation. Interlocking forces kept matter in motion, and everything was predictable. Not everything might be known at this moment, but there was no doubt that everything would be understood eventually, using the established scientific method.

Put crudely, the world was largely seen as a collection of particles of matter in motion, hitting one another, like billiard balls on a table, and behaving in a predictable way. It was thought that science would eventually give an unchallengeable explanation for everything, and that it would form the basis for technology that would give humankind increasing control over the environment, and the ability to do things as yet unimagined. Science became cumulative – gradually expanding into previously unknown areas; building upon the secure foundations of established physical laws.

Newton was a religious believer; he thought that the laws by which the universe operated had been established by God. But his god was an external creator who, once the universe had been set in motion, could retire, leaving it to continue to function according to its fixed laws. This view freed science from the need to take God into account: it could simply examine the laws of nature, and base its theories on observation rather than religious dogma.

With the coming of the Newtonian world-view, the function of philosophy changed. Rather than initiating theories about cosmology, the task of philosophy was to examine and comment on the methods and results of scientific method, establishing its limits. Kant, for example, argued that space, time and causality – the very bases of Newtonian science – were not to be found 'out there' in the world of independent objects, but were contributed by the mind. We saw things as being in space and time because that was the way our minds process the information given through the senses.

Hume pointed out that scientific laws were not true universal statements, but only summaries of what had been experienced so far. The method used by science – gathering data and drawing general conclusions from it – yielded higher and higher degrees of probability, but could never achieve absolute certainty.

Insight

Science always needs to be open to the possibility of contrary evidence – something utterly unexpected, requiring us to reconsider and perhaps modify our theories. Theories are therefore always provisional and limited.

Some aspects of philosophy related to this phase of science have already been examined (in Chapter 1). Hume's empiricism, for example, fits perfectly with the scientific impetus. At the beginning of the nineteenth century, William Paley's argument in favour of a designer for the universe (explained further on p. 163) reflects the domination of his world-view by the paradigm of the machine – a designer (God) is proposed in order to account for the signs of design in creation.

But not all philosophers supported Newton's fixed mechanical universe. Bishop Berkeley criticized Newton's idea that space and time are fixed. For Berkeley, everything (including matter and extension) is a matter of sensation, of human experience. Thus everything is relative to the person who experiences it, and there is no logical way to move from the relativity of our experience to some external absolute. In his own way, Berkeley anticipates the arrival of the third era for science and philosophy.

TWENTIETH-CENTURY DEVELOPMENTS

For most thinkers prior to the twentieth century, it was inconceivable that space and time were not fixed: a necessary framework within which everything else could take place.

Einstein's theories of relativity were to change all that. The first, in 1905, was the theory of *Special Relativity*, best known in the form of the equation E = mc². This showed that mass and energy are equivalent, and that (since energy was equal to mass multiplied by the speed of light squared) a very small amount of matter could be converted into a very large amount of energy. This, of course, is now best known for its rather drastic practical consequences in the development of nuclear weapons.

Einstein published the second theory, *General Relativity*, in 1916. It made the revolutionary claim that time, space, matter and energy were all related to one another. For example, space and time can be compressed by a strong gravitational field. There are no fixed points. The way in which things relate to one another depends upon the point from which they are being observed.

An example

Imagine you are looking out through space. You see two stars, which, although they may appear to you to be at the same distance, are in fact many light years apart. Suppose you see a change in one of those stars, followed by a change in the other. You might reasonably claim that one happened first, because from your perspective they occurred in a time sequence which, on Earth, would amount to one coming first and the other second.

But imagine that you are transported to a star that is beyond the second of the stars you have been observing. In this case you might see the second change first and the first change second. Clearly, the reason for this is that the time at which something 'happens' (or, strictly speaking, appears to happen) is related to the distance it is from you, because events only come to be observed after the light from them has travelled across space.

Of course, you could calculate which 'actually' happened first, from your perspective, if you knew the distances to the two stars. You could then calculate the extra length of time it took light to travel to you from the further star, and deduct that from the time difference between the two experienced events. But it would still be 'from your perspective', not absolute.

Modern physics and cosmology therefore offer a strange view of space and time, a view that is in contrast to that of Newton. We are told that the whole universe emerged (at the 'big bang') from a space-time singularity – a point at which all the matter of the present universe was concentrated into a very small point. Unlike an ordinary explosion, in which matter is propelled outwards *through* space, space and time were created at that moment, and space expanded as did the universe. If space could be represented by a grid of lines drawn on a balloon, then as the balloon is blown up, the grid itself expands, the balloon doesn't simply get more lines drawn on it.

The reason Newton's physics worked on the basis of fixed space and time was that he considered only a very small section of the universe, and within that section, his laws do indeed hold true.

Space and time are seen as linked in a single four-dimensional space–time continuum, and there is no fixed point from which to observe anything, for observer and observed are both in a process of change, moving through time and space.

Alongside relativity came quantum mechanics, which raised questions about whether events at the sub-atomic level could be predicted, and what it means to say that one thing causes another. Matter was no longer thought to be composed of solid atoms, but the atom itself was divided into many constituent particles, held together by forces. In the sub-atomic world, particles did not obey fixed rules. Their individual movements, while statistically predictable, were uncertain. Energy was seen to operate by the interchange of little packets or 'quanta', rather than by a single continuous flow. What had once been solid matter obeying fixed mechanical laws, could now be thought of as bundles of events open to a number of different interpretations depending on the viewpoint of the observer. Quantum mechanics is notoriously difficult to understand. A general view of it is that it works, so there must be something right about it, even if we don't understand it as a theory. What is certain is that quantum mechanics, however little understood, when combined with the theories of Relativity, rendered the old Newtonian certainties obsolete. Newton's laws of physics might still apply, but only within very limited parameters. Once you stray into the microscopic area of the sub-atomic, or the macroscopic world of cosmic structures, the situation is quite different.

Insight

A basic philosophical question: What can we mean by scientific 'truth' in such a strange, flexible and relativistic world?

A similar revolution has taken place within the understanding of living things. Through the discovery of DNA, the world of biology is linked to that of chemistry and of physics, since the instructions within the DNA molecule are able to determine the form of the living being.

In the twentieth century, therefore, philosophy engaged with a scientific view of the world that had changed enormously from the mechanical and predictable world of Newton. In particular, science started to offer a variety of ways of picturing the world, and cosmology – which had been dominated first by religious belief and Aristotle, and then by astronomy – was now very much in the hands of mathematicians. It became clear that the world as a whole was not something that could be observed; its structures could only be explored by calculation.

During much of the first half of the twentieth century, philosophy (at least in the United States and Britain) became dominated by the quest for meaning and the analysis of language. It no longer saw its role as providing an overview of the universe – it left that to the individual scientific disciplines. Rather, it adopted a supportive role, checking on the methods used by science, the logic by which results were produced from observations, and the way in which theories could be confirmed or discredited.

In other words

▶ *Up to the sixteenth century, Greek concepts, backed by religious authority, determined the general view of the world. Evidence was required to fit the overall scheme.*

> ▶ In Newtonian physics, matter exists within a fixed structure of space
>   and time, and obeys laws that can be discovered by 'induction' based
>   on observation.
> ▶ The modern world view sees space and time as related to one another,
>   and events as interpreted in the light of the observer's own position
>   and methods of observation.

Insight

In the first phase, philosophy seemed to determine content, in
the second it offered a critique of method, and in the third it
offered a clarification of concepts.

From evidence to theory: scientific method

In terms of the philosophy of science, the most important
approach to gathering and analyzing information was the 'inductive
method'. This was championed by Francis Bacon, and then by
Thomas Hobbes (1588–1679) and became the basis of the Newtonian
world of science. In its practical approach to sifting and evaluating
evidence, it is also reflected in the empiricism of Hume (see p. 21).
Indeed, it was the inductive method that distinguished 'modern'
science from what had gone before, and brought in the first of the
two major shifts in world view.

THE INDUCTIVE METHOD

This method is based on two things:

1 *The trust that knowledge can be gained by gathering evidence
   and conducting experiments, i.e. it is based on facts that can
   be checked, or experiments that can be repeated.*
2 *The willingness to set aside preconceived views about the
   likely outcome of an experiment, or the validity of evidence
   presented, i.e. the person using this method does not have a
   fixed idea about its conclusion, but is prepared to examine
   both results and methods used with an open mind.*

With the inductive method, science was claiming to be based on objectively considered evidence, and was therefore seen as in contrast to traditional religion and metaphysics, which was seen to be based on doctrines that a person was required to accept and which were backed up by authority rather than reason alone.

In practice, the method works in this way:

- *Observe and gather data (evidence; information), seeking to eliminate, as far as possible, all irrelevant factors.*
- *Analyze your data, and draw conclusions from them in the form of hypotheses.*
- *Devise experiments to test out those hypotheses, i.e. if this hypothesis is correct, then certain experimental results should be anticipated.*
- *Modify your hypothesis, if necessary, in the light of the results of your experiments.*
- *From the experiments, the data and the hypotheses, argue for a theory.*
- *Once you have a theory, you can predict other things on the basis of it, by which the theory can later be verified or falsified.*

It is clear that this process of induction, by which a theory is arrived at by the analysis and testing out of observed data, can yield at most only a high degree of probability. There is always the chance that an additional piece of information will show that the original hypothesis is wrong, or that it applies only within a limited field. The hypothesis, and the scientific theory that comes from it, is therefore open to modification.

Theories that are tested out in this way lead to the framing of scientific laws. Now it is important to establish exactly what is meant by 'law' in this context. In common parlance, 'law' is taken to be something which is imposed, a rule that is to be obeyed. But it would be wrong to assume that a scientific law can dictate how things behave. The law simply describes that behaviour, it does not control it (as Hume argued). If something behaves differently, it is not to be blamed for going against a law of nature, it is simply that either:

▶ *there is an unknown factor that has influenced this particular situation and therefore modified what was expected, or*
▶ *the law of nature is inadequately framed, and needs to be modified in order to take this new situation into account.*

Insight

To point out that all theories that are based on the inductive method are open to the possibility of modification is a *positive*, rather than a negative comment. This method is a hugely important feature of science, and one that delivers usable results.

FALSIFICATION

It may sound illogical, but science makes progress when a theory is falsified, rather than when it is confirmed, for it is only by rejecting and modifying a theory, to account for new evidence, that something better is put in its place. This view was argued very effectively by Karl Popper (1902–94), an Austrian philosopher from Vienna, who moved to New Zealand in 1937 and then to London in 1945, where he became Professor of Logic and Scientific Method at the London School of Economics. He was a socialist, and made significant contributions to political philosophy as well as the philosophy of science.

In his book *The Logic of Scientific Discovery* (1934, translated in 1959) Popper makes the crucial point that science seeks theories that are logically self-consistent, and that can be falsified. He points out that a scientific law goes beyond what can be experienced. We can never prove it to be absolutely true; all we can do is try to prove it to be false, and accept it on a provisional basis until such time as it is falsified.

This leads Popper to say that a scientific theory cannot be compatible with all the logically possible evidence that could be considered. It must be possible to falsify it. If a theory claims that it can never be falsified, then it is not scientific. On this basis, he challenged the ideas of both Marx and Freud.

In practice, of course, a theory is not automatically discarded as soon as one possible piece of contrary evidence is produced. What happens is that the scientist tries to reproduce that bit of contrary evidence, to show that it is part of a significant pattern that the theory has not been able to account for. Science also seeks out alternative theories that can include all the positive evidence that has been found for the original one, but also includes the new conflicting evidence.

An example

In Newtonian physics, light travels in a straight line. (This was confirmed over the centuries, and was therefore corroborated as a theory.)

But modern astronomy has shown that, when near to a very powerful gravitational field, light bends.

This does not mean that the Newtonian view was entirely wrong, simply that light does indeed travel in a straight line when in a uniform gravitational field. The older theory is now included within a new one which can take into account these exceptional circumstances.

Where you have a choice of theories, Popper held that you should accept the one that is not only better corroborated, but also more testable and entailing more true statements than the others. And that you should do this, even if you know that the theory is false. Since we cannot, anyway, have absolute certainty, we have to go for the most useful way of understanding the world that we have to hand, even if its limitations have already been revealed.

Insight

The implication of this would seem to be that science takes a pragmatic rather than an absolute approach to truth.

NEW EVIDENCE?

A theory should not necessarily be ignored just because present evidence fails to be conclusive, since we do not know what might come to light in the future. A theory may survive when it adapts to new situations yielding new evidence – a kind of **natural selection** in the scientific world.

A particularly appropriate example of this may be Charles Darwin's theory of natural selection. Darwin published *The Origin of Species* in 1859. He observed that within a species there were slight variations, most of which gave no particular benefit to the individual who displayed them. Sometimes, however, a beneficial variation gave that individual an advantage and, in a world of limited resources of food and habitat, the advantaged individual was more likely to survive to adulthood and breed. Hence, the beneficial variations would be passed on to a proportionately larger number of the next generation, and so on. Thus a competitive natural environment was doing exactly what a breeder of domestic animals would do in selecting and breeding individuals who showed particular qualities.

He presented natural selection as a process that he considered to be the best explanation for the variety of species that he had observed and catalogued.

Darwin thus claimed to have discovered the mechanism by which species evolve, and also an explanation of those features of each species which seem most appropriate to its own survival. His theory seemed to render obsolete the idea that the appearance of design in nature could only be explained by the existence of a designer God. In effect, natural selection explained how nature could design itself. Its implications were far beyond his areas of research. If species are not fixed, then everything is subject to change. To accept such an idea (with all its scientific, social, emotional and religious implications) on the basis of limited evidence was to take a great risk.

Insight
The theory of natural selection illustrates how a strictly inductive method of scientific argument, gathering and interpreting evidence, can then take an imaginative leap in order to grasp a more general theory.

But the debates that followed the publication of Darwin's theory were not simply about his perceived challenge to religious ideas, but about his interpretation of evidence. In particular, there did not seem to be adequate fossil evidence for a gradual evolution of species. In other words, the fossil evidence lacked sufficient 'halfway' stages that might illustrate the change from what appeared to be one fixed species to another. And, of course, weighing such evidence was an essential feature of the inductive method.

Today, we have evidence to support the theory of natural selection that was unavailable to Darwin. So, for example, in a book entitled *The Beak of the Finch* (1994), Jonathan Weiner described a 20-year study of finches on one of the Galapagos Islands, showing, for example, that in times of drought only those finches with the longest beaks could succeed in getting the toughest seeds, and therefore survived to breed. At the same time DNA studies of blood from various finches corresponded to their physical abilities and characteristics.

New evidence for survival of those best able to adapt to their changing environment is seen all the time in terms of medicine and agriculture. As soon as a pesticide appears to have brought a particular pest under control, a new strain is found which is resistant to it. Equally, in medicine, new strains of disease are appearing which are resistant to the available antibiotics. What is happening is that those examples of a pest or a disease which survive the onslaught of a pesticide or treatment, breed. The next generation is therefore resistant. These examples show the flexibility of nature: the present disease has been 'designed', not by some original designer but in response to existing treatments. We see an evolution of diseases over a space of a few years, mirroring the longer term evolution of species over millennia.

More generally, we now know that random genetic mutations are the cause of the tiny variations which form the basis of natural selection. Genetics therefore provides a whole new level of evidence. Analysis of the genetic make-up of each species is able to show how closely those species are related and may trace them back to common genetic ancestors.

There is no way that Darwin could have considered his theory from the standpoint of genetic mutation, or from the way in which viruses adapt and take on new forms, but such new areas of evidence may be used to corroborate a previously held theory, particularly where (as was the case with Darwin) the problem was not so much that his theory had been falsified as that there was a perceived lack of positive evidence.

Experiments and objectivity

Karl Popper argued that science was not subjective, in the sense of being the product of a single human mind, but neither was it literally objective, (i.e. a scientific law is not an external 'fact', but a way of stating the relationship between facts as they appear to us). Rather, it transcends the ideas of particular individuals, as does art, literature or maths. So how do the theories we devise, based on evidence and experiment, relate to what is 'out there' in the world?

The process of induction is based on the idea that it is possible to get hard evidence which does not depend upon the person who observes it. Indeed, from Francis Bacon onwards the theory has been that a scientist sets aside all personal preferences in assessing data. But can we observe nature without influencing it by our act of observing it, and how much of what we think of as evidence is contributed by our own minds?

The sensations that we have are not simply copies of external reality, they are the product of the way in which we have encountered that reality: colour is the result of a combination of light, surface texture and the operation of our eyes; space is perceived as a result of our brain linking one thing to another; time is a matter of remembering that some experiences have already taken place. Our experiences (and any theories based on them) are not independent facts, but the product of our ways of looking and thinking.

Kant argued that when we observe something, our mind has a contribution to make to that experience. Space, time and causality are all imposed on experience by the mind in order to make sense of it. Physics, since Einstein, has endorsed this relevance of the observer for an understanding of what it observed. As we saw above, neither space nor time is fixed, and movement is only perceived in terms of the change in position of one body in relation to another.

An example

I look out of the window of a stationary train at the train in the next platform. Suddenly, what I see starts to move. But is my train moving forward, or is the other train pulling away? Unless I feel a jolt, it will be a moment before I can decide between the two – and I will be able to do so only by looking beyond or away from the other train to some third object.

What is perceived transcends the individual perceiver, simply because the perception may be confirmed by others. Several people all witnessing the existence of a table in the room will confirm my own perception. In the same way, scientific evidence, repeated in various experiments, gives a trans-personal element of truth, even if the object being studied, and the way in which it is described, ultimately depend upon human perceptions.

Right, wrong or what?

The Newtonian world was at least predictable. A law of nature could be regarded as a fixed piece of information about how the world worked. That has now gone. We find that science can offer several equally valid but different ways of viewing the same phenomenon. There are no absolutes of space or time. Quantum theory is seen to work (results can be predicted on the basis of it) but without people understanding exactly why.

An example

Light can be understood in terms of particles or in terms of wave motions. They are two utterly different ways of understanding the same thing, but the fact that one is right does not mean that the other is wrong.

As laws and theories become established within the scientific community, they are used as a basis for further research, and are termed 'paradigms'. Occasionally there is a paradigm shift, which entails the revision of much of science. In terms of cosmology, the move from an Aristotelian (Ptolemaic) to a Newtonian world view, and then the further move from that to the view of Einstein, represents two shifts of paradigm.

Science offers a set of reasoned views about how the world has been seen to work up to the present. Taken together, the laws of science that are understood at any one time provide a structure within which scientists work; a structure which guides and, influences, but does not dictate how scientific research will progress. With hindsight, we can see philosophers and scientists boldly proclaiming the finality of their particular vision of the world just as the scientific community is about to go through a 'paradigm shift' as a result of which everything is going to be re-assessed.

An example

In 1899, Haeckel published *The Riddle of the Universe*. He argued that everything, including thought, was the product of the material world and was controlled by its laws. Everything was absolutely controlled and determined. Freedom was an illusion and religion a superstition. He was proposing scientific materialism, popularizing Darwin's theory of evolution, and sweeping away all earlier philosophy that did not fit his material and scientific outlook. For Haeckel, science had discovered just about everything there was to discover; there would be no more surprises. What would he have made of relativity, quantum theory, genetics or computing?

T.S. Kuhn, in his book *The Structure of Scientific Revolutions* (1962), described these paradigms as the basic *Gestalt* (or world view) within which science at any one time interprets the evidence it has available. It is the paradigm that largely dictates scientific progress, and observations are not free from the influence of the paradigm either.

What makes Kuhn's theory particularly controversial is that he claims that there is no *independent* data by which to decide between competing paradigms (since all data is presented either in terms of one paradigm or the other) and therefore there is no strictly logical reason to change a paradigm. This implies a relativism in science, which seemed to threaten the logical basis of the development of scientific theories, as expounded by Karl Popper.

The general implication of the work of Kuhn and others is that, if a theory works well (in other words, if it gives good predictive results), then it becomes a *possible* explanation: we cannot say that it is *the definitive or only one.*

In other words

▶ *Different theories can give an equally true explanation of the same phenomenon.*
▶ *A scientific theory is a way of looking: a convenient way of organizing experience, but not necessarily the only one. It is provisional. It is also part of an overall paradigm.*

Imre Lakatos (1922–74) particularly argued that science is generally carried out within research programmes, and is essentially a problem-solving activity. There are core theories within a research programme (without which the whole programme would fail) and a 'protective belt' of theories that are more open to modification, while continuing with the overall programme. Core theories are not simply abandoned at the first piece of contrary evidence. At any one time, there will be many research programmes on the go, and they are gradually modified in a way that is rather more subtle than a straight 'falsificationist' view might suggest.

But beyond that, there are other criteria for assessing theories. 'Instrumentalism' is the term used for the evaluation of a theory on the basis of whether or not it actually works in making valuable predictions. Hence a theory may be useful, even if we are unable to say whether or not it is right.

If one scientific theory continues to be regarded as 'right' (however provisional it may be) does this imply that alternative theories must be 'wrong' or what? This is a question for the philosophy of science: Can we say that something is 'right' in a world of optional viewpoints?

The social sciences

Humankind is clearly a valid object of study for science. When Darwin published *The Origin of Species*, much of the controversy that followed was generated because his theory of natural selection applied to humankind as well as all other species, and that was seen as particularly threatening of the special place accorded to the human species in most traditional religious and philosophical thinking. In more recent debates, Richard Dawkins (in *The Selfish Gene* and elsewhere) examines the relationship between human behaviour and life at the genetic level, where genes are inherently 'selfish', in that their task is simply to promote survival and to reproduce successfully. It is also possible to show that human behaviour can be examined alongside, and in the same way as that of other species, as Edward Wilson did in his controversial book *Sociobiology*.

There are, however, particular problems when science examines humankind. First of all, there continues to be a widespread view that science is basically determinist. In other words, setting aside the subtleties and developments that we have already examined in this book, it sees science as giving a single, fixed and empirically based explanation of every phenomenon. On the other hand, the experience of being human – the subjective side of what science examines objectively – is of freedom, complexity, mixed motives and so on. In spite of philosophers like Kant, who were quite able to see us as being phenomenally determined (as seen by others) but noumenally free (as experienced in ourselves), most people have found it difficult to accept any scientific attempt to 'explain' human life at either a social or individual level.

On the other side of the argument, two disciplines in particular – sociology and psychology – have sometimes had their methodologies and findings challenged by the mainstream physical sciences. We shall therefore look at each of these briefly, to see what special issues they raise for the philosophy of science.

SOCIOLOGY

The scientific method relies on measurable data. Today, we are accustomed to statistical information about humankind, from life expectancy and income to our shopping preferences and voting intentions. But it was only in the nineteenth century that information began to be gathered and presented in the form of statistics. Before that, philosophers made observations about humankind in general, but were unable to move from those observations to produce scientifically based theories about society.

Most widely known of the early sociologists was Emile Durkheim (1858–1917). He analyzed regularities in society and formed theories to explain them. Although each individual was aware of a measure of freedom over his or her actions, the assumption upon which Durkheim worked was that there were social forces at work, as real as physical forces, which influenced behaviour. These forces put pressure on individuals to conform, and the number of individuals influenced would then show up in statistics.

Insight

Statistics tell me that, if I am male and under the age of 30, I am more likely than an elderly female to drink and drive, or take illegal drugs. But do those statistics actually influence me to do either of those things? I am free to choose, and so is everyone else. I can say, 'Well, life just happens to be like that!' But that is exactly what a sociologist is claiming, that certain features of human life can be quantified and examined in a scientific manner.

On the political side, Karl Marx (1818–83), as a result of researching social and political patterns in societies over history, formulated his theory (dialectical materialism) that social activity is based on people's material needs and the means of producing and distributing them. He saw evidence for a pattern within society, in which classes oppose one another, and thus drive forward a process of social and political change.

As has already been discussed, some thinkers (e.g. Popper, see p. 47) question whether Marxist theory should be considered to be genuine science, on the grounds that Marx appears to interpret evidence in the light of an overall theory, whereas Popper sees genuine science as always open to the possibility that a theory will be falsified and replaced.

Nevertheless, it is clear that sociology and political science are valid disciplines, operating using methods that are not that far removed from the physical sciences. They are based on the interpretation of data, gathered using the normal checks to obtain objectivity. One major difference between these disciplines and, say, physics is the scope for conducting experiments. Because human beings are involved, it is perfectly valid to collect data about their behaviour, but it is not considered ethical to subject them to intrusive testing that may cause them harm. Hence (in spite of the present interest in reality shows on television) it would not be acceptable to send a bunch of people into an extreme environment to measure who died first and from what!

PSYCHOLOGY

Sigmund Freud (1856–1939) was a hospital doctor with a particular interest in neuro-pathology, later setting himself up as a private practitioner for the treatment of nervous conditions, particularly hysteria. As is well known, he developed the method known as psychoanalysis in which, through dream analysis and free association, patients were encouraged to become aware of those experiences buried in their unconscious which were having a harmful effect on their conscious behaviour. So, for example, examining those who had compulsive washing routines, he sought the origin of the compulsion in buried childhood experience of uncleanness. Psychoanalysis worked on the assumption that, once the origin of a problem was discovered and articulated, it would lose its power, and the patient would be cured.

Psychoanalysis depends on the analytic skills of the practitioner. What the patient says is analyzed and given significance, and that analysis is done in the light of the overall theory and approach of the analyst. Notice here the old problem for the philosophy of science – which comes first, the data or the interpreting theory? Popper criticized Freud as much as Marx, on the grounds that their work did not have the scientific discipline that allowed their theories to be open to falsification.

Other branches of psychology are more in line with traditional scientific method. Behaviourism, for example, set up animal experiments, and thus produced data that could be analyzed in much the same way as in the physical sciences. However (as we shall see in Chapter 4) there are issues about the validity and scope of behaviourism as a way to understand human behaviour. By being more traditionally scientific in its method, it limited what it could examine. Measuring the ability of a rat in a box to learn how to press a lever in order to get food, is hardly likely to explain the sort of compulsive neuroses that interested Freud!

Cognitive science is a major area of research today, and we shall examine it again in Chapter 4. For now we only need to note the basic fact that the study of humankind, whether in sociology, psychology or cognitive science, presents a special set of problems for the application of traditional scientific method.

What counts as science?

At one time, an activity could be called 'scientific' if it followed the inductive method. On these grounds, the work of Marx could be called scientific, in that he based his theories on accounts of political changes in the societies he studied. Similarly, behavioural psychology can claim to be scientific on the basis of the methods used: observing and recording the responses of people and animals to particular stimuli, for example. So science is generally defined by method rather than by subject.

Popper criticized both Marx and Freud, not because he considered they failed to observe and gather evidence, but because of what he saw as their willingness to interpret new evidence in the light of their theories, rather than to allow that evidence to challenge or modify those theories. So how should we distinguish between science and what Popper called 'pseudo-science'?

An example

Astronomy is regarded as a science. Astrology, on the other hand, is not. This is because the former is based on observable facts, while the latter is based on a mythological scheme.

Except: suppose astrologers could show that there was a definite link between a person's star sign and his or her behaviour. Suppose the results of a very large number of studies indicated this. Would that prove that astrology was scientific?

On the face of it, it would probably depend upon who did the experiment; if it were an attempt to gather favourable information to support the previously held views, then it would not be acceptable. On the other hand, if it were gathered in a strictly objective way, by someone who genuinely wanted to know if the phenomena of star signs was relevant to human behaviour, then it might be claimed to be scientific.

But even if it were shown to have a scientific basis, astrology would only be termed a science if its practitioners subsequently used scientific methods of assessment and prediction.

Distinguishing features of science include the consistent attempt at the disinterested gathering of information and the willingness to accept revisions of one's theories. But what happens if one's conclusions are radically different from those of other scientists? This leads us to ask about the nature of authority within the scientific community.

Science and authority

With the rise of science in the seventeenth and eighteenth centuries, it was widely believed that the days of superstition and authority were over; everything was to be considered rationally. But has that always been the case with the discipline science?

Once a theory, or a method of working, has become established, the scientific world tends to treat it as the norm and to be rather suspicious of any attempt to follow a radically different approach. When Darwin introduced the idea of natural selection, or Einstein the theory of relativity, the radical changes in scientific outlook that they implied were seen by some as a threat to the steady accumulating of knowledge along the previously accepted ways of seeing the world. Although both were accepted, there was a pause for consideration.

Scientists may be considered to be 'heretics' within the world of scientific orthodoxy, if their views are radically different from those of the majority of their peers.

Since it is possible that there will be different but equally valid theories to account for phenomena, there will always be an element of debate within scientific circles. But are there limits to the range of views that can be accommodated within the scientific community?

An example

The chemist Linus Pauling claimed that vitamin C was a panacea that could not only cure colds, but could help resist cancer and prevent heart disease. In spite of the recognition of his work on molecular structures, for which he had received a Nobel Prize, his views on this were generally dismissed by the scientific community, although they became popular with the general public.

New scientific work is presented to the world scientific community by being published, generally in one of the established 'peer reviewed' journals. In order to be accepted for publication, of course, it must be plausible as a piece of work, at least to those who are reviewing it. Once published, the theory may be evaluated by other scientists. The original experiments are repeated elsewhere to see if the same results can be obtained. Sometimes the results of attempting this are ambiguous; sometimes the attempt to repeat the experiment failed completely, and the validity and reliability of the original results are then called into question.

An example

In 1989, two chemists, Martin Fleischmann and Stanley Pons, claimed to have achieved a breakthrough in the quest for cold nuclear fusion – the possibility of creating unlimited supplies of energy by creating nuclear fusion (merging atoms together, as opposed to the usual way of generating nuclear energy by fission – splitting atoms apart – which produces heat and radiation as well as radioactive waste). But fusion, the process that powers the sun, normally only happens at extreme temperatures generated in particle accelerators, and even then the amount of energy generated by fusion is only a fraction of the amount taken to generate those extreme conditions. If it were found that cold nuclear fusion were possible using seawater, as Fleischmann and Pons suggested, it would revolutionize the production of energy.

This was received with a degree of scepticism, on the assumption that there must be something wrong with an experiment if its results are so much at variance with existing scientific understanding, and although their experiments were studied and repeated many times by other scientists, they failed to give any positive confirmation. However, that does not mean that research into nuclear fusion is over. In 2005, it was announced that a new $12 billion international research centre into nuclear fusion was to be built in France, and in 2009 scientists from California published a paper on the analysis of neutron tracks in an experiment that seemed to suggest that cold nuclear fusion had taken place. Particular methods and results may thus be challenged as part of an ongoing quest.

Scientists have to earn a living. Some are employed by universities and are therefore, in theory, free to explore their theories without external influence – other than the requirement that they show real advance in research in order to continue to attract funding. On the other hand, the funding for such research often comes from the commercial world, and is not, therefore necessarily totally disinterested.

Other scientists are employed within various industries. Their task is to find a scientific basis and make possible the enterprise which their industry seeks to promote. They are not engaged in 'pure' science (in the sense of a quest for knowledge, unfettered by its implications) but science put to the use of industry. Their task is halfway between science and technology – they seek a basis upon which a technology can be developed in order to achieve something that will then yield a profit.

An example

A scientist employed by a drugs company is hardly likely to keep his job if his conclusion is that the disease he is attempting to combat by the development of a new drug is best cured by drinking pure fruit juice!

He or she is therefore likely to try the following:

▶ *isolate the element within the fruit juice which actually effects the cure*

(Contd)

Commercial funding looks for new products and ideas for developing those things in which it has a vested interest, and even state funding favours those projects that promise economic benefit. Philosophers like Bacon and Hume insisted that the quest for knowledge should be a disinterested one. Indeed, the fact that a scientist stands to gain a great deal from a particular conclusion to his or her research might indicate that the results should be treated with some caution. We have already seen that there are really no facts that are free of interpretation and this flexibility, coupled with a personal motive, makes the tendency to incline towards the most favourable conclusion a real threat to impartiality.

FOR REFLECTION

What can be said about the world, and what cannot? In *Tractatus* (see p. 71), Wittgenstein took the view that the function of language was one of picturing the world and started with the bold statement, 'The world is everything that is the case' (*Tractatus* 1) and equates what can be said with what science can show, 'The totality of true propositions is the whole of natural science' (*Tractatus* 4.11).

It ends, however, with the admission that when it comes to the mystical (the intuitive sense of the world as a whole) language fails; we must remain silent. What is 'seen' in a moment of mystical awareness cannot be 'pictured'. It cannot be expressed literally.

Wittgenstein points to other things that cannot be described – the subject self (it sees a world, but is not part of that world) and even death (we do not live to experience death). Wittgenstein is thus setting limits to what can be said, and by implication, limits to science.

His thought might prompt us to ask:

▶ *Is not modern cosmology a bit 'mystical'? Does it not seek to find images (including that of the 'big bang') by which to express events so unlike anything experienced on Earth, that literal language is of little use?*

▶ *Does science not sometimes require imaginative leaps beyond evidence, in the formation of new paradigms, within which detailed work and calculation can subsequently find its place?*

▶ *What is the place of intuition within the scientific process? Like an eye which sees everything other than itself, intuition may underpin much of the scientific endeavour without itself ever featuring directly.*

Science offers a very rich and exciting view of the world. Whether you start by considering the idea that matter is a collection of nuclear forces, rather than something solid and tangible, or whether you start with the idea that the universe is expanding outwards from the space-time singularity, creating its own space and time as it does so, modern science seems to contradict our common-sense notions. Yet, in doing so, it performs the valuable function of shaking us out of our ordinary assumptions and reminding us that the world is not as simple as may at first sight appear. In this, science acts rather like philosophy: challenging our assumptions and examining the basis of what we can say about reality.

In other words

▶ *Philosophy cannot determine what information is available to science: it cannot provide data.*

▶ *Philosophy examines the use of scientific data, and the logical processes by which this information can become the basis of scientific theories.*

▶ *Most importantly, philosophy can remind scientists that facts always contain an element of interpretation. Facts are the product of a thinking mind encountering external evidence, and they therefore contain both that evidence and the mental framework by means of which it has been apprehended, and through which it is articulated.*

Science is not confined to theoretical knowledge; it has practical consequences. Through the products of technology, science raises ethical issues – from genetic engineering to nuclear weapons – and this brings it into contact with another branch of philosophy to be considered later in this book: ethics. Science may show what is possible, and technology may make it possible, but that does not address the issue of whether the use of that technology is right or wrong. Just because you can do something does not mean that it is right to do it. Thus, whereas the philosophy of science is concerned with the validity of scientific method, science itself has implications in other areas of thought, including ethics and the philosophy of mind.

10 THINGS TO REMEMBER

1 *Science was originally called 'natural philosophy'.*

2 *Science is characterized by method, rather than by results.*

3 *Science is based on evidence and experiment, rather than pre-established theory.*

4 *The inductive method attempts to get objective conclusions from empirical data.*

5 *Science progresses as existing theories are falsified and replaced.*

6 *Science generally works within an accepted 'paradigm'.*

7 *There may be more than one valid theory to explain a phenomenon.*

8 *New evidence may validate previously neglected theories.*

9 *Theories are subject to peer review and acceptance by the scientific community.*

10 *Science is influenced by funding priorities and has ethical implications.*

3

Language and logic

In this chapter you will learn:
- *about the function of different forms of language*
- *about how language may be assessed and its claim verified*
- *about formal logic and the limitations of rational discourse.*

Language is the vehicle through which the ideas and concepts of philosophy are transmitted. It might be tempting therefore to assume that it has a necessary but secondary role, communicating what is already known. But that would be mistaken, for philosophical issues arise within, and often as a result of our language. A basic question in philosophy is, 'What do we mean by ... ?' which asks for more than a definition – it seeks to relate the thing we are interested in to the rest of our ideas and language. The language we use colours the way in which we think and experience the world.

It is therefore most unwise to philosophize without being aware of the role played by language. In looking at language, however, there are three quite different things to examine:

▶ *the* **philosophy of language** *(which looks at what language is, how it works, whether statements are meaningful and how it may be verified)*
▶ **linguistic philosophy** *(which is a way of doing philosophy through the analysis of problematic statements)*

▸ **logic** *(which examines the structure of arguments, in order to illustrate whether their conclusions can be shown to follow from their premises).*

Language and certainty

A key question for the study of language is **'verification'**. How can you show that a statement is true?

▸ *Do you set out bits of evidence that correspond to each of the words used? (An empiricist might encourage you to do that. A reductionist might say that your statement was nonsense unless you could do it!) This assumes that language has a picturing or pointing function.*

▸ *Is a statement 'true' if its logic is sound? If so, does its truth also depend on some sort of external evidence?*

The distinction between 'synthetic' and 'analytic' statement has already been made. But language is complex: an average line of poetry, a joke, a command, a piece of moral advice or the whispered endearments of lovers can quickly dispel any simple theory of verification. We need to move on from 'Is it true?' to the broader issue of 'What, if anything, does it mean?'

In examining the quest for certainty in Chapter 1, we looked at Descartes (who cannot doubt his own existence as a thinking being) and at the empiricist approach. We also saw the way in which Kant identified the contribution of the mind to our process of understanding the world, and went back to Plato, noting the way in which, for him, the world of appearances is but a shadow play, and that reality is in the world of 'Forms'. If we do not know exactly what the world is like, how can we know if our language reflects it accurately?

Probably the greatest influence in shaping modern life is science, which (as we saw in Chapter 2) is based on observation of the world, and uses empirical data to form hypotheses. With the obvious success of science, it was very tempting for philosophers to see science as in some way a paradigm for the way in which knowledge as a whole could be gained.

As science is based on observation, each claim it makes is backed up with reference to data of some sort. Without data, there is no science. The language used by science is therefore justified with reference to external objects. It 'pictures' them. A statement is true if it corresponds to what has been observed, false if it does not so correspond. But can this test be applied to all language?

LOGICAL POSITIVISM

Ludwig Wittgenstein (1889–1951), an Austrian who did most of his philosophy in Cambridge and studied under Bertrand Russell, was deeply impressed by the work done in mathematics and logic by Gottlob Frege (1848–1925), Russell and A. N. Whitehead, with whom Russell had written *Principia Mathematica*, a major work attempting to establish the logical foundations of mathematics. These thinkers had argued that logic and mathematics were objective, not subjective; that is, they described features of the external world, rather than simply showing ways in which the mind worked.

Wittgenstein suggested that philosophical problems would be solved if the language people used corresponded to the phenomenal world, both in terms of logic and the evidence for what was being said. In the opening statement of his hugely influential book *Tractatus* (1921), he identifies the world with the sum of true propositions: 'The world is all that is the case', but he has to acknowledge that there are therefore certain things of which one cannot speak. One of these is the subject self: 'The subject does not belong to the world; rather it is a limit of the world.' Another is the mystical sense of the world as a whole. Whatever cannot be shown to correspond to some observable reality, cannot be meaningfully spoken about.

His ideas were taken up by the Vienna Circle, a group of philosophers who met in that city during the 1920s and 1930s. The approach they took is generally known as **logical positivism**. Broadly, it claims that:

▶ *Analytic propositions tell us nothing about the world. They are true by definition, and therefore tautologies. They include the statements of logic and mathematics.*

▶ *Synthetic propositions depend on evidence. Therefore there can be no necessary synthetic propositions.*

▶ *Metaphysics and theology are literally 'meaningless' – since such statements are neither matters of logic (and therefore true by definition – a priori) nor are they provable by empirical evidence.*

Moritz Schlick, one of the Vienna Circle, argued that 'the meaning of a statement is its method of verification'. This became known as the 'Verification Principle'.

Logical positivism was promoted by the British philosopher A. J. Ayer (1910–89) in an important book entitled *Language, Truth and Logic* (1936). In that book he asks: 'What can philosophy do?' His answer is that it certainly cannot tell us the nature of reality as such – in other words, it cannot provide us with metaphysics. If we want to know about reality we have to rely upon the evidence of our senses.

He therefore argued that philosophy cannot actually give new information about anything, but has the task of analysis and clarification. It looks at the words people use and analyzes them, showing their logical implications. By doing so, philosophy clarifies otherwise muddled thought.

He argued that every genuine proposition, capable of being either true or false, should be either a tautology (in other words, true by definition) or else an empirical hypothesis (something which makes a claim that can be verified by experience). He therefore considered all metaphysics to be meaningless, for its claims involved statements that were neither capable of empirical verification, nor true by definition.

Of course, there are other kinds of meaning, but Ayer is concerned with statements which claim to have 'factual meaning'. In other words, if experience is not relevant to the truth or falsity of a statement, then that statement cannot claim to have factual meaning, whatever else it may claim by way of meaning of significance for the person making it.

Ayer distinguished between two forms of what can be called the Verification Principle:

1 *A proposition is said to be verifiable and have meaning if and only if its truth may be established in experience. This is the strong form of the Verification Principle, as originally proposed by Moritz Schlick: meaning and verification are identical.*

An example of the strong form

'There are three people in the next room.'

Meaning: If you go into the next room, you will see three people there.

2 *A proposition is said to be verifiable if it is possible for experience to render it probable, or if some possible sense experience would be relevant to determining whether it was true or false. This weaker version was the one Ayer himself favoured. Clearly, it is not always possible to get factual evidence – about the past, for example, or about events predicted to happen in inaccessible places. Where evidence is simply not available, it was thought important at least to be able to specify what sort of evidence would count for or against the factual truth of such a statement.*

Statements are meaningless if there is nothing that would count for or against them being true. On this basis, much of what passes for religious language, or aesthetics, or morality, would be categorized as 'meaningless', because none of these things can be specified in terms of concrete facts that can be checked by observation.

If the only meaningful statement is one that is in the form of an empirical proposition, there is really nothing more to say. Ayer accepts that statements may be emotionally significant for him, but not literally significant – but it is literal significance which is taken to be the basis of certainty.

However, there are two fundamental problems with logical positivism and its verification principle:

1 *How do I know that what I think I see is actually there? I could ask other people to look, checking if they see the same thing. But that would never actually prove that the object was there – for there is no way of getting beyond the sense experiences to the thing-in-itself. However many bits of evidence I get, I can never have absolute proof that there is an external thing being observed: we could all be mistaken.*

Insight

In other words, if you base your certainty on evidence, you should also be aware that evidence is never certain!

2 *How do we verify the statement: 'The meaning of a statement is its method of verification?' Is it synthetic? If so, what is the evidence for it? What evidence could count against it? Or is it analytic? If so then the word 'meaning' is logically the same as 'method of verification' and the theory doesn't say anything.*

This second criticism sounds plausible, but is actually based on a false notion of what the Verification Principle claimed to do. It never claimed to be a factual proposition, rather it set out a policy for evaluating propositions which claimed to be factual, and that is a very different matter. After all, at a road junction a sign may tell you to turn right, but the sign itself does not turn to the right! An instruction is not the same thing as a statement of fact.

The key thing about logical positivism was that it represented a particularly strong form of empiricism and a particularly narrow form of language. The service it rendered philosophy was that, by arguing that a wide range of propositions was 'meaningless', it forced philosophers to think again about the way in which we use language. Whereas the logical positivists had concentrated on a simple 'picturing' view of language, it was soon realized that language can be meaningful in terms of many other functions (for example: expressing feelings; giving commands; stating preferences). In this way, by reacting against the logical positivists, it became widely recognized that a more sophistical view of the function of language needed to be developed.

That said, the Verification Principle is a valuable check, to make sure that statements about personal preferences or commands do not parade themselves as though they were straightforward empirical statements of fact.

Interestingly, towards the end of his life (as illustrated by the interview extract on p. 26), Ayer was to admit that his thought had moved on since the time of writing *Language, Truth and Logic* (accepting that one might communicate aesthetic experience, for example); but that book remained an important touchstone for a particular view of language and approach to philosophy.

Few today would want to take on the bold claims of meaning and certainty of the logical positivists or Ayer, since philosophy has in general recognized the far more flexible nature of language, but they came from a period when science and mathematics were generally thought to provide suitable images of clarity and precision, and therefore became models of an approach to which ordinary language was pressed to conform.

But where does that leave general statements about the way the world is?

Language and perception

In what sense can a proposition be known to be true? In the Introduction, we saw that statements could be true by definition or true by experience. The former included statements of mathematics. Once the words were known, the truth or falsity of a statement followed automatically.

But as we looked at statements based on experience, we found other problems. First of all, there is the uncertainty about any experience: it might always be mistaken or interpreted differently. Secondly, there is the way in which we have to use general words in order to describe particular things:

▶ *Imagine a situation in which there were no general words. How would you describe a tree without the word 'tree', or without the words 'green', 'tall' or 'thick', etc.? Each of these words, unlike a proper name, has a meaning which can be applied to a whole variety of individual things – indeed, learning a language is about learning the whole range of general terms which we can put together in order to describe particular things.*
▶ *Do these general terms refer to things that exist, or are they simply 'names'? Does 'goodness' exist, or is it just a name for certain kinds of things of which I approve? We saw this reflected in differences between Plato and Aristotle, and in the realists/nominalists debate.*

- *In looking at logical positivism, we saw a philosophy that was based on the 'picturing' function of language. Statements had meaning only if they reflected evidence (or potential evidence) from the world of the senses.*
- *But how far can we trust our perception? And is perception the same thing as sense data?*

It's all a matter of interpretation

There are a number of examples of drawings that can be interpreted in a number of different ways. Here is a simple example:

Do you see the profiles of two people facing one another, or do you see an elegant chalice?

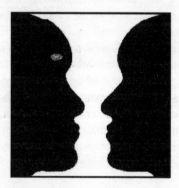

- *Try switching your perception from one to the other – notice the mental effort involved.*
- *Is there any difference between the one and the other perception – difference, that is, in what is actually being seen?*

Such visual games illustrate the ambiguity of all experience. As you make the mental effort to shift from one interpretation of what you see to the other, you are discovering the reality of 'experience as' – that all experience requires an element of interpretation.

Here is the dilemma facing any empirical method of verification
for language:

▶ **If** *all experience involved 'experiencing as'*
▶ **And** *if two people may therefore interpret the same data
differently*
▶ **How** *do you decide between them or verify the truth
of what they say?*

> **Note**
>
> It seems curious that, in logical positivism, philosophy was
> developing a narrow view of meaning (that of picturing items of
> sense data) at the very time when science was starting to realize
> that there can be two different and incompatible ways of viewing
> things, both of which can be considered correct, as with the wave
> or particle theories of light.

Knowledge and language

As far as philosophers in the Anglo–American tradition were
concerned (see Chapter 8 for the different approach taken by
Continental philosophy), for much of the twentieth century,
philosophy was dominated by the discussion of language. Indeed, there
was a feeling that this was all that philosophy was about – everything
else being sorted out by sciences or politics or sociology. Philosophy,
rather than having any specific content, was an activity, and that
activity was to do with the sorting out of words and their meaning.

So philosophy was given a role rather like that of an indigestion tablet, something necessary in order to purify the system and enable comfort and efficiency to return. *Philosophy, according to that view, would help every other subject by clearing away its linguistic confusions.*

Early in the twentieth century, as we previously saw, the logical positivists argued that the meaning of a statement was its method of verification. This view attempted to purge language of all that could not be reduced to sense experience. Metaphysics was out, and ethics was little more than the expression of a preference.

By the 1950s this view of language was becoming broader. Wittgenstein (who, in the earlier phase of his work, had espoused this radically reductionist approach to language) broadened his view, and accepted that language could take on different functions, of which straight description of phenomena was only one. This allowed greater flexibility, and recognized that the expression of values and emotions, the giving of orders and making of requests, were all valid uses of language. His keynote was that language was a 'form of life' and that, to understand it, it had to be observed in use.

He described the different uses of language as 'language games'. Just as a game, such as chess, can only be appreciated once the rules for moving the various pieces are understood, so language can only be understood within its context; words have meaning that is related to their function in the 'game'. This is not to trivialize language (it is not a 'game' in that sense), but to recognize that language is a tool for doing something – a tool that is based on rules that are understood by those who use it.

At this point, philosophers seemed to be catching up with common sense, and abandoning the purity of the unchallengeable statement as the goal of meaning. To know the meaning of a statement, you have to see it in its context and understand what it is intended to achieve. In Chapter 6 we shall be examining different tasks that language can perform in the field of ethics. What we need to recognize at this point is that language is neither simple nor transparent.

In other words

▶ *People (hopefully) think before they speak.*
▶ *They may also perceive before they think.*

Therefore

▶ *What they say reflects the nature of thought and of perception.*
▶ *Language is therefore only as simple and straightforward as the thought and perception that produced it.*

Add intuition, emotion, existential angst and the general confusions of human life, and the resulting language is very complex indeed.

▶ *It may perform many different functions.*
▶ *It may play many different games.*
▶ *We may not even be aware of the implications of what we are saying, which is to return to Plato, who in his dialogues portrays Socrates as a man who is constantly asking people what they mean, and thereby exposing their confusions and opening up the way to greater clarity.*
▶ *Without language we cannot have metaphysics or epistemology: indeed, we cannot have philosophy, civilization, culture or other distinctively human features of life.*

Linguistic philosophy

While the logical positivists were analyzing statements in terms of their verification through sense experience, other philosophers – notably, G. E. Moore (1873–1958) and J. L. Austin (1911–60) – were investigating the ordinary use of words. Along with the broader approach taken by Wittgenstein, this led to the view that ordinary speech was an activity that could be analyzed to show its internal logic and implications, and that such analysis would clarify meanings and therefore solve philosophical problems.

This approach, known as 'linguistic philosophy', became a dominant feature of philosophy in the 1940s and 1950s. In Chapter 4 we shall see that one of the most controversial books on the Philosophy of Mind at the time was entitled *The Concept of Mind*, and offered a radical view of mind based on the analysis of ordinary language.

And here is the key to what linguistic philosophy was about: it worked on the assumption that philosophical problems came about because of the ambiguities and confusions of normal speech. Once that speech could be analyzed and its confusions exposed, new insights and clarity would emerge.

Linguistic philosophy therefore redefined the task of philosophy in terms of the clarification of language. We see linguistic philosophy having a significant influence on the philosophy of mind (in asking what we mean when we use words like 'mind' or 'person'), or ethics (where moral statements can be considered in terms of recommending a course of action, for example). It is a way of doing philosophy, and it is not the same as the philosophy of language, which asks questions about how language develops, what it does and how it relates to those things which it describes or brings about, and how it is learned.

Insight

As a student, I found linguistic philosophy clever but frustrating – it was all to do with the subtleties of meaning and apparently nothing to do with life. That has largely changed, with philosophy engaging directly with issues in ethics, politics and personal identity, rather than simply analyzing the language used.

Formal logic

Logic is the branch of philosophy which examines the process of reasoning. When you start with a set of premises and reach a conclusion from them, the process of doing so is called **deductive logic**. An argument is *valid* if it is impossible for the conclusions to be false if the premises are true. An argument can be valid even if the premises are false (and therefore the conclusion is false); just because you are mistaken, it does not mean that your reasoning is not logical. An argument where the premises are true and the logic is valid is *sound*.

Logic has a long history. In Plato's dialogues we find Socrates debating with various people. He invites them to put forward propositions and then analyzes their implications and the arguments they have used. His argument often takes the form of, 'If B follows from A, and B is clearly wrong, then A must also have been wrong.'

But the main influence on logic for 2,000 years was Aristotle. He set down the basic features of deductive logic, in particular the **syllogism**, in which major and minor premises lead to a conclusion.

The most quoted piece of logic ever, has to be the syllogism:

All men are mortal.
Socrates is a man.
Therefore Socrates is mortal.

This can be expressed as:

All As are B.
C is an A.
Therefore C is B.

From the basic syllogism, we can go on to explore the forms of *inference* – in other words, what can validly follow from what.

Some principles of logic appear quite obvious, but are crucially important for clarifying arguments. William of Ockham (1285–1349), a logician who commented on Aristotle, is best known for his argument that one should not multiply entities unnecessarily. In other words, given a number of possible explanations, one should incline towards the simplest. This is generally known as *Ockham's Razor*.

Logic is often able to highlight common errors. One of these is known as the *argumentum ad ignorantiam*, which is to argue for something on the grounds that there is no evidence *against* it, whereas to establish that something is the case, one needs to show evidence for it.

In other words

There may be no evidence that someone did not commit a particular crime, but that cannot be offered as proof that he or she did commit it. If this basic feature of logic were overlooked, the justice system would be in deep trouble. Notice that an *argumentum ad ignorantiam* may sometimes be slipped into a popular discussion of the paranormal: there is no evidence to show that extra-terrestrials were not the cause of some phenomenon, therefore, in the absence of any other explanation, we can take it that they were!

Logic can become very complex, with parts of an argument depending on others: 'if not this, then that, but if that then something else … '. Clearly, it would be cumbersome to write out all the elements of each argument in order to examine the logic involved.

To overcome this problem, formal logic uses an artificial form of language. This language uses sets of letters, A, B, C, etc., to stand for the various component premises and conclusions, and also a set of signs to act as connectives. These signs stand for such logical steps as 'and', 'or', 'it is not the case that', 'if … then' and 'if and only if'.

This use of artificial languages is particularly associated with the German philosopher and mathematician Gotlob Frege (1848–1925).

> ## Example
>
> The connective 'if … then' is shown by an arrow pointing to the right. The conclusion (therefore) is shown as a semi-colon.
>
> Take this argument:
>
> I have missed the train. If I miss the train I arrive late at work. Therefore I shall arrive late at work.
>
> We can formalize this by using the letter 'A' for 'I have missed the train' and 'B' for 'I will arrive late at work'.
>
> Rewritten, the argument becomes:
>
> A (A → B); B

An important feature of logic is that it breaks down each sentence into its component parts and makes clear the relationship between them. So formal logic helps to clarify exactly what is and what is not valid. Arguments set out in this way become very complex indeed, and there are a large number of unfamiliar signs used for the various connectives. If you pick up a copy Russell and Whitehead's famous *Principia Mathematica* or browse through *The Journal of Symbolic Logic* you will see page after page of what looks like advanced mathematics or complex scientific formulae. For the uninitiated, it is extremely difficult to follow!

MATHEMATICS

Much work on logic has been done by mathematicians, and that is not surprising, since mathematics, like logic, works on premises and rules. Two philosophers already mentioned, Frege and Russell, independently came to the conclusion that the rules of mathematics could be shown to be elementary logic, and that it should therefore be possible to *prove* the basis of mathematics. In their work, developed by Russell in *Principia Mathematica* (published in three parts, 1910–13), mathematics becomes an extension of logic, and in theory (although not in practice, because it would take far too long to set down) all mathematical arguments could be derived from and expressed in logical form.

Earlier, we saw that statements may be categorized as synthetic (depending on experience and therefore uncertain) and analytic (known directly and therefore certain). Now where does mathematics fit into this scheme?

A classic example of an analytic statement is $2 + 2 = 4$. One does not have to check numerous examples to come to the conclusion that their sum will always be 4 and never 5. This is true in general of mathematics; it is a matter of logical deduction and certainty. But does that mean that mathematics is true only in the mind? Is it not the case that two things, added to another two things in the external world, will always make four? If this is so, then things in the 'real' world can be understood through mathematics and logic; *it has to do with actual relationships, not simply with mental operations.*

Insight

If this were not so, how is it that theories about the origin of the universe come from professors of mathematics?

Perhaps, like so many other issues, this can be traced back to Plato. He held that numbers, or geometrical shapes such as triangles or squares, were all perfect; you don't get 'almost square's or a 'nearly 2' in mathematics. But in the real world, nothing is quite that perfect. He therefore held that mathematics is about objects known through the mind rather than the senses, objects which (like his 'Forms') belonged to a world different from the one we experience. Hence, mathematics could be known a priori, with a certainty impossible with things in this world.

Predictably, Aristotle countered this with the claim that mathematical concepts were abstractions and generalizations, based on things experienced. The debate between the Platonic and Aristotelian views has been very influential in the history of mathematics, as in so many other areas of philosophy.

The philosophy of mathematics is a major area of study, beyond the scope of this book. All we need to note is the close relationship between mathematics and logic. Debate continues into whether arithmetic can validly be reduced to 'set theory' and whether mathematics as a whole can fully be reduced to logic and, if so, what the value is in making such a reduction.

IN DEFENCE OF THE ILLOGICAL

Just because Frege saw that mathematics was based on logic, and logic is concerned with the structure of language, it does not follow that all language is (or should be) presented with mathematical precision, any more than the logical positivists succeeded in eliminating all statements that could not be empirically verified. At the very end of *Tractatus*, Wittgenstein pointed out that there were some things of which one had to remain silent. In other words, they were beyond the scope of meaningful propositions, validated with reference to sense experience. But that has not stopped people speaking of them.

Language performs a great variety of functions, and its meaning is given by its function. When we move on to examine Continental philosophy – including existentialism and postmodernism – we shall be exploring questions about the meaning that do not fit the more narrow parameters of analytic philosophy. We have to be prepared to explore the fact that a statement can communicate something of importance, even if – by the standards of an Aristotelian syllogism – it is illogical.

This is not to make a value judgement, simply to point out that logical argument is not the only form of meaningful language.

10 THINGS TO REMEMBER

1   *Logical positivism sought to model all meaningful language on science, picturing the world.*

2   *It saw religious, ethical and aesthetic language as factually meaningless.*

3   *The strong form of the Verification Principle identifies meaning with the method of verification.*

4   *The weak form equates meaningfulness with the ability to specify what could count as evidence.*

5   *Perception (and the language in which it is expressed) depends on interpretation.*

6   *Wittgenstein later argued that meaning was shown by use.*

7   *Wittgenstein also argued that meaning was given within the rules of a 'language game.'*

8   *Linguistic philosophy seeks to solve problems by clarifying language.*

9   *Formal logic analyzes arguments using a shorthand notation.*

10 *Language need not be logical in order to be meaningful.*

4

....

The philosophy of mind

In this chapter you will learn:

- *some theories about how our minds relate to our bodies*
- *about artificial intelligence and how it compares with human thought*
- *about how we get to know ourselves and one another.*

> *It was on a dreary night of November, that I beheld the accomplishment of my toils. With an anxiety that almost amounted to agony, I collected the instruments of life around me, that I might infuse a spark of being into the lifeless thing that lay at my feet. It was already one in the morning; the rain pattered dismally against the panes, and my candle was nearly burnt out, when by the glimmer of the half-extinguished light, I saw the dull yellow eye of the creature open; it breathed hard, and a convulsive motion agitated its limbs.*
>
> *Frankenstein, 1818*

Thus Mary Shelley describes the moment of triumph and disaster for Victor Frankenstein in her novel. He had sought the origin of life by a process of analysis; dissecting the human body and exploring its various components. He had observed the changes that take place on death, the corruption of the various organs, and had longed to reverse that process, to bring life back to the dead. Then he collected the 'materials' for his experiment – all the various bits of human anatomy – and fashioned them into a human-like creature. Eventually he finds the secret of their animation, and in that horrifying moment, the creature which he has fitted together comes to life. (In Shelley's novel details of this process are not given, but later film treatments of the Frankenstein story have generally focused on electricity, the spark of life being brought about by the sparks of electrical discharge.)

Released into the world, the 'creature', not fully human and shunned by society, nevertheless develops human emotions, reasoning and skills. Filled with both tenderness and rage, longing for a mate of his own kind and murderously angry with Frankenstein for creating him thus, he asks 'Who am I?'

The 'philosophy of mind' (sometimes called 'philosophical psychology'), is that branch of philosophy which undertakes the Frankenstein-like task of analyzing bodies, minds and persons, dissecting them and attempting to re-animate them, in order to understand the nature of intelligent life.

As you read this book, your eyes are scanning from left to right, your fingers turn the pages, your brain is consuming energy, taking oxygen from its blood supply, tiny electrical impulses are passing between brain cells. All that is part of the physical world, and can be detected scientifically. How does all that relate to the process of reading, thinking, learning and remembering? And how do both relate to personal identity?

If, as the result of an accident, I were to have an arm or leg amputated, I should refer to the detached member as 'my arm' or 'my leg', not in the sense that I owned it, but that I regarded it as part of myself, a part which I must now do without. In the same way, I can list all the parts of myself: my hair, my face, my body, my mind, my emotions, my attitudes. Some of these will be parts of my mental make-up, others will be parts of my physical body.

Where in all this is the real 'me'?

▶ *Am I to be identified with my physical body?*
▶ *Am I my mind?*
▶ *Could I exist outside my body?*

- *If so, could I continue to exist after the death of my body?*
- *Is my mind the same thing as my brain?*
- *If not, then where is my mind?*
- *Can I ever really know other people's minds, or do I just look, listen and guess what they're thinking?*
- *What about computer-created artificial intelligence?*

These are just some of the questions that are explored within the philosophy of mind. Its issues relate to biology, psychology, sociology, computer science, and all aspects of human thought, memory, communication and personal identity.

Ancient minds: Plato and Aristotle

We have already looked at Plato's idea of the 'Forms' – the eternal realities by which we are able to understand and categorize the particular things that we encounter. He argued that, since they are eternal and cannot be known through the senses, we must have had knowledge of them prior to birth, and hence that there is an eternal element to the self. But, if so, how is it related to the physical body?

It is possible to trace a development in Plato's thinking on this through the various dialogues, and it is clear that he wanted to take into account both knowledge of the eternal realities and also the fact that individuals are shaped by the environment into which they are born – so the self cannot be entirely separate from the body.

In *The Republic*, Plato describes the self by way of analogy with a city. Just as a city has workers who produce its goods and services, the military who organize and defend it, and an elite of philosopher-guardians who rule it, so the self has three parts: the physical body with its appetites, the spirited element which animates and drives it, and the thinking mind that rules it. For Plato, the ideal is to have the appetites held in check by the active faculties, which are in turn guided by reason. In other words, he sees the ideal human life as integrating its three distinct elements in a hierarchy.

Aristotle's approach was very different. He rejected Plato's idea
of the immortal self, but he was equally critical of the idea that
the self was some kind of material substance. His great work on
this is *On the Soul* (*De Anima*). Aristotle argued that everything
had both physical substance and form (or essence). The form of
something is what makes it what it is. To use his own example, you
take some wax and give it a particular shape by using a mould or
stamp. How does the shape relate to the wax? There is no shape
without wax. But, at the same time, the shape is not the same thing
as the physical wax that forms it. In the same way, Aristotle sees
the self (or soul) as the form or essence of the physical body. It is
not something that is separable from the body (you don't have a
shape if you don't have any wax), but it is not the same thing as
the body. To use another of Aristotle's analogies, an eye is not the
same thing as 'seeing', but you cannot see without an eye, and if
the eye cannot 'see', then it is not an eye – for the essence of an
eye is 'seeing'.

Naturally, both Plato and Aristotle have far more to say about the
nature of the self, but this contrast between the two of them sets
the agenda for much later debate about the relationship between
the self and the physical body. However, their views have been
overlaid by that of another philosopher to whom we must now
turn – Descartes.

'I think, therefore I am'

In looking at the theory of knowledge, we found that Descartes –
using the method of systematic doubt in his quest for certainty – could

doubt everything except his own existence as a thinking being. Hence his key statement: 'I think, therefore I am.' This provided him with a starting point from which to build up knowledge. But it also created an absolute distinction between the physical body (which is extended in time and space and which can be known to the senses), and the mind (which is not extended, and which has one function – to think).

So, while Plato can speak of a physical body, with an animating self, ruled by a thinking self, and while Aristotle sees the self as that which gives form and purpose to the physical body, Descartes absolutely pulls apart the physical and the mental – the one is in the world of space and time, the other is not.

In the next section we shall examine the general question of the relationship between mind and body, an issue with which the philosophy of mind was much preoccupied from the time of Descartes up to the second half of the twentieth century. In doing this we will need to return again to both Plato and Descartes, since they both argued for a form of **dualism**. However, in looking at the various forms of dualism, it is worth keeping the historical perspective in view – Cartesian dualism is not the same as that of Plato, and it is only with developments in cognitive science in the latter part of the twentieth century that we return to a broader appreciation of the complexity of the mind/body issue which – following Descartes – had been focused on the single 'problem' of how a non-physical mind could influence a physical body.

The relationship between mind and body

Philosophy has explored a whole range of possible relationships between mind and body. At one extreme there is the view that what we call 'mind' is simply a way of describing the physical body and its activities (**materialism** and **behaviourism**), at the other is the rarer idea that everything is fundamentally mental (**idealism**). Between these is the view that both bodies and minds have distinct but related realities (**dualism**). How exactly they are related is a further problem, and so our consideration of dualism has many sub-theories.

MATERIALISM

A materialist attempts to explain everything in terms of physical objects, and tends to deny the reality of anything that cannot be reduced to them. So, for a materialist, the mind or 'self' is nothing more than a way of describing physical bodies and their activity. We may experience something as a thought or an emotion, but in fact it is *nothing but* the electrical impulses in the brain, or chemical or other reactions in the rest of the body.

Note

This 'nothing but' is an example of the philosophical approach known as '**reductionism**' – the view that the reality of each thing lies in its simplest component parts, rather than the whole phenomenon of which they are parts. Reductionism would suggest, for example, that:

▶ *music is nothing but a set of vibrations in the air*
▶ *a painting is nothing but a collection of coloured dots on canvas*
▶ **so** *a person is nothing but a brain, attached to a body and nervous system.*

The 'nothing but' distinguishes materialism from other theories, for nobody would deny that, in some sense, a person is related to a brain, in the same way as a symphony is related to air movements. The essential question is whether or not it is possible to express what a 'something more' might be, if the materialist position seems inadequate.

Points to consider:

▶ *Apply electrical shocks to the brain, and the personality can be affected. (This is the basis of a form of treatment for severe depression, simulating epileptic fits.)*

▶ *A person who suffers brain damage is no longer the same. In severe cases he or she may not appear to be a person at all, but merely a living body, devoid of all the normal attributes of mind.*

Do these examples confirm the materialist view?

For reflection

You see people waving to you and smiling.

▶ *Does this indicate that they are friendly? That they know you? That they have minds as well as bodies? That they have freely chosen to act in that way? That they have previously recognized you, had friendly thoughts towards you, and therefore decided to wave?*

▶ *Let us analyze what is actually happening as you look at one of those people:*

  ▷ *You see an arm moving.*
  ▷ *Within that arm, muscles are contracting.*
  ▷ *The contraction is caused by chemical changes, brought about by electrical impulses from the brain.*
  ▷ *The electrical activity in the brain has caused the impulses.*
  ▷ *That activity depends on consuming energy and having an adequate oxygen supply via the blood.*
  ▷ *Nutrition and oxygen are taken in from the environment.*
  ▷ *And so on, and so on …*

(Contd)

> ▶ *The act of waving is explained in terms of a material chain of cause and effect. That chain is, for practical purposes, infinite – it depends upon the whole way in which the universe is constructed. There is no point in that chain for some 'mind' to have its say. The world, as we experience it through the senses, appears to be a closed system, within which everything is totally determined by physical causes and conditions.*

Behaviourism is the term used for the rather crude materialist theory that mental phenomena are in fact simply physical phenomena. Crying out and rubbing a part of the body is what pain is about. Shouting and waving a fist is what anger is about. All mental states are reduced by the behaviourist to things that can be observed and measured.

Insight

Behaviourism developed out of the desire for a scientific approach to the mind that could involve measurement and experiment. Rats in cages learned to press a lever to get food, and dogs to salivate at the bell rung before its arrival. Behind behaviourism lay the thought that human minds too could be controlled by adjusting their environment and by conditioning.

The problem is that we experience a difference between a sensation or thought and the physical movement or the words that result from it. I can think before I speak, or before I write, but for a behaviourist there is nothing other than the words or the writing. To know a feeling, for a behaviourist, one must observe behaviour. This might be a plausible theory if one is observing rodents in a cage, but becomes more problematic when human beings are concerned. One can, for example, observe a brilliant performance by an actor – and one knows it to be a brilliant performance because it gives an illusion of (but is clearly not the same as) the expression of genuine emotions and views. But how, if everything is reduced to what is being observed, can one ever even contemplate the idea of being fooled by someone else about their real feelings? We shall examine this and related problems later in this chapter.

IDEALISM

George Berkeley's idealist theory of knowledge has already been considered in Chapter 1 (see p. 19). All that we know are the ideas in our mind, and we have to infer the physical world from them. What we speak of as 'body' is simply an aggregation of mental facts that are our interpretation of the data that emerge from our sense organs.

A criticism of the idealist approach might be that, although we may not be certain of the existence of matter, for all practical purposes we have to assume it. However much our knowledge of other people is the result of our interpretation of the sense impressions we receive, we are forced by common sense to infer that there really are people with minds and bodies like our own. One of the key problems of a strictly idealist approach is that it leads to **solipsism** – the view that we are unable to know other minds, forever locked in the lonely contemplation of our own sense experience. Perhaps understandably, idealism has not been a popular approach to the issue of how mind and body are related.

DUALISM

If neither the materialist nor the idealist position convinces you by its account for the relationship between mind and body, the answer may be sought in some form of dualism: that mind and body are distinct and very different things. Each is seen as part of the self, part of what it means to be a person, but the question then becomes: How do these two things interact?

This question has a long history. Plato, in *Phaedo*, argued for the immortality of the soul on two grounds:

1 *That the body was composite, and was therefore perishable, whereas the mind was simple, and therefore imperishable.*

2 *That the mind had knowledge of the universals – the eternal Forms (such as 'goodness' or 'beauty') – but its experience during this life is of individual events and objects. Hence Plato argued that the soul itself must be immortal, having existed in the realm of the Forms before birth, and thus also able to survive the death of the body.*

Few people today would wish to take up these arguments in the form that Plato presented them. But they persist in two widely accepted features of the mind/body question:

1 *That the mind is not within space/time and not material – and thus that it should not be identified with its material base in the brain.*
2 *That the mind functions through communication – it is not limited to the operations of a single particular body, i.e. the mind is not subject to physical limitations, and is related to a network of transpersonal communication.*

For reflection

Where does our conversation take place? Within my mouth? Within yours? Somewhere in the space between us? Or is a conversation not related to space in the same way as physical bodies? We know that a conversation is going on in a room, for example, which gives a broad physical location, but not a specific one. Try asking where the internet is located and you start to run into exactly the same problems. Every piece of information is actually contained on some physical computer somewhere, but the overall effect is of a reality that is not physically limited.

Descartes' starting point in the quest for knowledge, 'I think, therefore I am', implied a radical distinction between the world of matter, known to the senses, and the mental world, known (at least in one's own case) directly. They are two different realms, distinct but interacting. The mind, for Descartes, is able to deflect the flow of physical currents in the nervous system, and thus influence the mechanical working of the physical body. For Descartes, there has to be a point of interaction, for in all other respects he considers the material world to be controlled by mechanical forces, and without a mental component to make a difference, there would be no way in which a mental decision to do something could influence that otherwise closed mechanical world.

One danger here is to imagine the mind as some kind of subtle, invisible body, existing in the world of space and time, yet not subject to its usual rules of cause and effect. This, of course, is a rather crude caricature of what Descartes and other dualists have actually claimed.

Insight

It is also an important caricature, having been used by Gilbert Ryle in *The Concept of Mind* (1949), an influential book for an understanding of the mind/body issue, where he called the Cartesian dualism the 'official view' and labelled the mind 'the ghost in the machine'.

The essential thing for Descartes is that mental reality is not empirical and therefore not in the world of space. The mind is not located in the body – it may be related to the body, but is not some occult alternative set of physical causes and effects. It is therefore a matter of debate whether Ryle was justified in calling Descartes' view 'the ghost in the machine', although a popular form of dualism may well give that impression.

Forms of dualism

EPIPHENOMENALISM

This view is that the brain and nervous system are so complex that they give the impression of individuality and free choice. Although totally controlled by physical laws, we therefore 'seem' to have an independent mind. This is the closest that a dualistic view comes to materialism. The essential thing here is that the mind does not influence the body – the mind is just a product of the complexity of the body's systems.

The various things that I think, imagine, picture in my mind are epiphenomena. They arise out of and are caused by the electrical impulses that move between brain cells, but they are not actually part of that phenomenon, they are above (epi-) them.

For reflection

When does epiphenomenalism start to become thinkable?

Imagine a robot, programmed by a computer. A simple version could be the source of amusement, as it attempts to mimic human behaviour. But as the memory capacity of the computer is increased, the process of decision making in the program is so complex that an observer is no longer able to anticipate what the robot will select to do, and the robot (via the computer) gradually starts to take on a definite personality or character of its own. In this case the character that starts to emerge is seen to be a product of the computer's memory, and hence it would be an epiphenomenon. (We shall examine artificial intelligence later in this chapter.)

INTERACTIONISM

Most forms of dualism claim that the mind and the body are distinct but act upon one another. For example, if you have tooth decay (a bodily phenomenon) it will lead to pain (a mental experience); the body is affecting the mind. Equally, if you are suddenly afraid, you may find yourself breaking out in a cold sweat and start to shake; the mind is affecting the body. Although they interact, the mind and body remain distinct and appear self-contained. Thus (to take up the example of the person waving) an interactionist would not try to claim that there was some break within the series of causes that led to the arm waving. The physical world remains a closed system within the body, but *the whole of that system is influenced by the mind*, and responds to its wishes.

But how exactly is this interaction to come about? Here are some theories:

Occasionalism:

> On the occasion of my being hit over the head with a cricket bat, there is a simultaneous but uncaused feeling of pain! The two systems (physical and mental) do not have a direct causal connection. The philosopher Malebranche suggested that whenever he wanted to move his arm, it was actually moved by God.

Pre-established harmony:

> The physical and mental realms are separate and independent processes. Each appears to influence the other, whereas in fact they are independent but running in harmony. This view was put forward by Geulincx, a Flemish follower of Descartes. It is also found in Leibniz, who holds that ultimately everything is divisible again and again until you arrive at monads – simple entities without extension, and therefore mental. These monads cannot act upon one another, for each develops according to its own nature. But a complex being comprises countless monads. How do they all work together to produce intelligent activity? Leibniz argued that there must be a pre-established harmony, organizing the otherwise independent monads. As far as human persons are concerned, Leibniz holds that there is a dominant monad (a soul) and that God has established that the other monads, which together form the complex entity that is a person, work in harmony with it.

Note

'Pre-established harmony' may seem to be one of the most bizarre of the mind–body theories, but for Leibniz it served a very specific purpose, and one which has important implications for

(Contd)

both metaphysics and the philosophy of religion. Leibniz was concerned to preserve the idea of **teleology** (i.e. that the world is organized in a purposeful way) in the face of the mechanistic science and philosophy of his day.

If everything is locked into a series of causes and totally determined by them, what room is left for a sense of purpose or for God? Leibniz' answer is that the individual monads of which everything is comprised do not actually affect one another. Rather, God has established a harmony by which they can work together.

DOUBLE ASPECT THEORY

This is the view, sometimes called the 'identity hypothesis', that the ideas a person has, and the operation of bits of his or her brain, are simply *two aspects of the same thing*. Thinking is thus the inner aspect of which the outer aspect is brain activity.

Insight

Perhaps we could use an analogy and say that music is the inner cultural aspect of which sound waves of particular frequencies are the outer physical aspect.

Of course, if the identity hypothesis is correct, there is a problem with freedom. Brain activity, like all physical processes, is limited by physical laws and is in theory predictable. But if mental events are simply another aspect of these physical events, they must also be limited by physical laws. If all my action is theoretically predictable, how can I be free?

Spinoza argued that everything is both conscious and extended; all reality has both a mental and a physical aspect. The mind and body cannot be separated, and therefore there can be no life beyond this physical existence. Spinoza also held that freedom was an illusion, caused by the fact that we simply do not know all the real causes of our decisions.

Survival?

The relationship between body and mind has implications for the idea that human beings might survive death.

If Plato was right to think that the soul was eternal, then its existence does not depend upon the physical body, and it is therefore at least logically possible for it to survive the death of the body. Similarly, Descartes' dualism of extended body and thinking mind at least leaves open the possibility of survival, since the mind is separate from the body, and cannot be reduced to anything physical.

However, if one accepts a materialist or behaviourist view of the self, it would make no sense to speak of a self that existed separately from a body, or survived physical death, since the self is an aspect of bodily activity. The only possibility would be to redefine death in some way, so that it allowed for some form of physical existence to continue, but that would beg the whole question about survival of death, since 'death' in the normal sense of the word would not have occurred.

From the religious point of view, belief in life after death is linked to two other fundamental ideas:

1 *There is a deeply held view that there should be some appropriate compensation, good or bad, for what a person has done during his or her life. All religious traditions have some element of reward or punishment, whether externally imposed (as in Western religions) or self-generated (as the 'karma' of Eastern traditions).*

2 *There is also a sense that human life somehow goes beyond the confines of a fragile human body, expressed in the idea that 'This cannot be everything: there must be something more.'*

Neither of these constitutes evidence for survival of death. What they do show is the appropriateness of such belief for a religious person, and the reasons why he or she might hold to it in the absence of evidence.

In terms of the religious perspective on survival, we should note that there are three different possibilities: immortality, resurrection and reincarnation.

Immortality implies that there is a non-physical element to the self that can exist independently of the physical body with which it is presently associated. This presupposes a dualist view of the mind/body relationship, and does not strictly speaking require belief in God, since a natural immortality can be argued as a logical consequence of dualism.

Resurrection, the Christian view, is that the soul is not naturally immortal, and that the whole person – body and mind – dies, but is then raised to life by God and given a new body. This view depends on a prior belief in God, assumes that individuality requires some sort of body in order to express itself, but raises many questions about the nature of an embodied future life. If that future life is to be endless, then what age is a person in such a future life? A body, after all, can vary from baby to old age. Would a resurrected child become the adult that he or she never was? Would I, in such a life, recognize my grandfather as a young man, and would he recognize me as an old one? This issue, of course, begs all the questions about knowledge of other minds and so on.

Reincarnation, particularly associated with Hindu philosophy, sees the soul as distinct from the body, and as able, at death, to move on to take up another physical body. Personal qualities and dispositions move on from life to life, expressed through a sequence of physical incarnations. Rather like the idea of resurrection, this assumes dualism (since the self that moves on is not the same as the physical body), but still considers the self to require some form of physical body in order to live.

Insight

Although illogical, the need to accommodate belief in an afterlife is without doubt a significant factor in shaping some people's view of the nature of the self. Materialism is really only an option for those who take a secular, atheist or a Buddhist view.

The concept of mind

Gilbert Ryle suggested, in *The Concept of Mind* (1949), that to speak of minds and bodies as though they were equivalent things was a '**category mistake**'. To explain what he meant by this he used the example of someone visiting a university and seeing many different colleges, libraries and research laboratories. The visitor then asks, 'But where is the University?' The answer, of course, is that there is no university over and above all its component parts that have already been visited. The term 'university' is a way of describing all of these things together – it is a term from another category, not the same category as the individual components.

In the same way, Ryle argued that you should not expect to find a 'mind' over and above all the various parts of the body and its actions, for 'mind' is a term from another category, a way of describing bodies and the way in which they operate. This, he claims, is the fundamental flaw in the traditional dualistic approach to mind and body (which he attributes to Descartes and calls the 'ghost in the machine'):

> **When two terms belong to the same category, it is proper to construct conjunctive propositions embodying them. Thus a purchaser may say that he bought a left-hand glove and a right-hand glove, but not that he bought a left-hand glove, a right-hand glove and a pair of gloves .... Now the dogma of the Ghost in the Machine does just this. It maintains that there exist both bodies and minds; that there occur physical processes and mental processes; that there are mechanical causes of corporeal movements and mental causes of corporeal movements. I shall argue that these and other analogous conjunctions are absurd; but, it must be noticed, the argument will not show that either of the illegitimately conjoined propositions is absurd in itself. I am not, for example, denying that there occur mental processes. Doing long division is a mental process and so is making a joke. But I am saying that the phrase 'there occur mental processes' does not mean the same sort of thing as 'there occur physical processes', and, therefore, that it makes no sense to conjoin or disjoin the two.**

> *The Concept of Mind, Peregrine Books, 1949, p. 23*

For Ryle, talking about minds is a particular way of talking about bodies and their activity. Remember, however, that Ryle is primarily concerned with language – his book is about what we mean when we speak about the 'mind'. What he shows is that, in ordinary language, mental terms actually describe activities performed by the body, or are at least based on such activities. We speak about the mind of another person without claiming to have any privileged information about their inner mental operations.

An example

If I say that someone is intelligent, I do so on the basis of what he or she has said or done. Descriptions of mental states depend upon information provided by physical bodies, activities and forms of communication.

▶ *Think of a person you know.*
▶ *Consider exactly what it is you mean when you describe that person's personality or mind. Think of particular qualities that you would ascribe to him or her.*
▶ *Consider the evidence you could give to back up your view of these qualities.*
▶ *Consider what would have to happen in order for you to be persuaded that you were mistaken about him or her.*

Clearly, we can get to know another person but, if Ryle is correct and there is no 'inner' self to be found, in what does the personality consist? His answer is in terms of 'dispositions'. These are the qualities that make me what I am; the propensity to behave in a particular way in a particular situation; the sort of beliefs and knowledge that habitually inform my actions and words.

If I say that someone is 'irritable' I do not mean that I have some privileged access to an 'irritability factor' in their mind. I just mean that, given a situation that is not to his or her liking, he or she is likely to start complaining, sulking, etc. In other words, the irritability is simply a way of describing a disposition.

Thus, for Ryle, the ascription of mental predicates (clever, etc.) does not require the existence of a separate, invisible thing called a mind. The description 'clever' may indeed refer to the way in which something is done but, equally, cleverness cannot be defined simply in terms of that action. What is clever for one person might not be so for another, and the mental description refers more to the way in which the individual person habitually relates to the world, and the expectation a person would have of him or her, rather than some special quality of an action that makes it clever.

One particular difficulty with identifying a mental phenomena with physical actions is illustrated by the idea of pain.

▶ *I may shout, cry, hold the afflicted part of my body; I may scream and roll on the ground, curl up, look ashen. But none of these things is actually the same thing as the pain I am experiencing. The pain is indicated by them, but not defined by them.*

▶ *I may watch an actor performing all the things listed above. But because he or she is acting, I do not imagine that there is any actual pain.*

▶ *Yet, if being in pain is actually identified with those things (as Ryle implies), then the actor is in pain.*

Comment

Much modern debate on the mind/body issue has been prompted by Ryle's critique of dualism. One feature of his work that one should keep in mind is that his approach is linguistic. He asks what it means to ascribe mental predicates. The question remains, of this or any similar approach, whether the meaning of the mental predicate is the same as its method of verification. I can verify my description of someone as clever by observing and listening to him or her. But is the information I receive in that way identical to what I mean by cleverness? Or is cleverness hinted at by, but not defined by, such information?

The real threat of Ryle's argument to those who wish to maintain the idea of an independent, separate 'soul' over and above the body, is that he shows that most of what we say about people and their personalities can be justified with reference to their words, actions and general dispositions. Hence, in ordinary discussion about people, the idea of a separate soul is redundant.

A 'place' for mind?

A basic question for mind/body, as for many other areas of philosophy: Can something exist if it does not have a place within the world of space and time?

It is clear, for example, following Ryle, that there is no place for a 'self' or 'soul' alongside the body. Everything to which language about the mind refers has its own place in the world – the clever action, the kindly word – and he is surely right to claim that the words 'clever' and 'kindly' here would not refer to some occult substance, but to the way in which particular deeds are performed.

But the dualist is not actually saying that the mind exists physically outside the body. The dualist position is that the mind is not extended, that it does not exist within time and space. We have returned therefore to the fundamental philosophical issue of reductionism. Consider any piece of music:

▶ *It comprises a sequence of sound waves within the air.*
▶ *There is no music apart from those sound waves. For even if I have a tune running in my head (a problematic thing for any philosopher to say) what I am doing is recalling that pattern of sound waves.*

- All the qualities of music (its ability to move one emotionally, its sense of beauty, of completeness, its ability to calm) have as their source that series of sound waves.
- The language a musician uses to describe a piece of music is quite different from the language a physicist uses to describe sound waves.
- There is no hidden, secret music that exists alongside the sound waves – rather, the sound waves are the physical medium through which music is generated.
- **Therefore** it really should not be too difficult to see that the brain, along with the nervous system and all the physical activities (including speech) that it controls, is the physical medium through which a mind expresses itself.

There have been many subtle variations on the problem of how the body and mind are related, but most of them can be seen, in one way or another, to be a result of an attempt to express the interconnectedness and yet distinctness of physical and non-physical reality.

What is clear from recent neurophysics is that the brain is extremely complex, that it controls not just the autonomic nervous system, but also those elements that we describe as personality or mind.

It is equally clear that an essential feature of the mind is communication. It is difficult to see how one could describe a mind that did not communicate – and in communicating, by words, facial expressions, writing, the qualities of that mind are shared. It is no more sensible to try to analyze an isolated human brain in the hope of discovering the seeds of cultural history, than it is to take a Stradivarius apart in order to discover why a violin concerto can be so moving!

BACKGROUND NOTES

A person's view on the mind/body issue depends on his or her general view of the world and knowledge of it. It is possible to trace the debate through the history of philosophy. For example:

- ▶ Plato sees the soul as eternal, trapped in a limited material body.
- ▶ Aristotle sees the soul as the 'form' of the body (everything for him has both substance and form), giving it unity.
- ▶ For Descartes ('I think therefore I am') the mind is primary.
- ▶ Hume said (in his 'Treatise on Human Nature'): '... when I enter most intimately into what I call myself, I always stumble on some particular perception or other, of heat or cold, light or shade, love or hatred, pain or pleasure. I never can catch myself at any time without a perception, and never can observe any thing but the perception.' Hume, an empiricist, cannot see a general 'self' because he cannot step outside the world of phenomena, which is his starting point for all knowledge.
- ▶ Kant argues that humans are phenomenally conditioned but noumenally free, therefore the mind is beyond the categories that apply to sense experience.

There is also a tradition which puts the mind quite beyond what can be known. So, for example, Wittgenstein, at the end of the *Tractatus*, says: 'The subject does not belong to the world, but it is a limit of the world.' In other words, from the standpoint of empirical evidence, I do not exist. As I experience it, the world is everything that is not me, although it includes my own physical body.

Insight

It is also possible to see the self as a process, rather than an entity – a process that unfolds as personal history, mapping out moments of personal significance. To follow up on this idea, see my book *Me* (listed in the Further reading section).

Neurones and computers

In *The Astonishing Hypothesis: The Scientific Search for the Soul* (1994), the scientist Francis Crick asked how it is that, if the brain is a machine made up of nerve cells and neurones, it can also take on the functions of what we know as mind: appreciating colour, telling jokes, thinking through problems. He argued that the brain had 'awareness neurones', which were the physical basis of mind, and that the 'soul' was physically located in the head, and therefore that research into brain activity would eventually reveal the processes which we call consciousness.

In suggesting this, Crick was rejecting two common conceptions. The first (from a dualistic standpoint) is that the soul or mind is not physically located in the body but is external, and may therefore be able to survive the death of the body. The second is the 'homunculus' idea: that the soul is distinct from the brain, but located inside the head, like a person within a person.

Instead, he argued that a complex structure has characteristics that go beyond those of its component parts. (So, for example, a city has a character over and above those of its individual citizens.) Therefore the 'soul', or mind, is the product of the interactions of the billions of brain cells. The human brain is, after all, the most complex thing known in the universe. Most of it controls the various functions that keep us alive, but he suggested that other parts of the brain could be involved with consciousness.

Notice what can and cannot be claimed by taking Crick's approach. 'Awareness neurones', once identified, could be recognized as the physical basis of mind, in exactly the same way that DNA is the physical and chemical basis of life. (Crick was awarded a Nobel Prize in 1962 for his part in the discovery of DNA.) Since the unique set of characteristics of any physical body is given in its DNA, we can identify an individual through its analysis. But that does not mean that the physical body is 'nothing but' a DNA code; the code is simply the set of instructions for building that unique body. In the same way, the most that Crick's quest for 'awareness neurones' might show is the physical location of mental activity. It cannot explain it.

In other words

▶ Our DNA does not show where we live, or what experiences we have had. It makes us unique, it enables all the cells in our body to grow

> *and work together, but it does not make us a 'person'. Traces of it*
> *in body tissue can identify us and show basic characteristics, but it*
> *cannot describe what we are like as living beings. Life is based on DNA;*
> *but life is not the same thing as DNA.*
>
> ▶ *Similarly, 'consciousness neurones' could not be 'you' any more than*
>   *your DNA is 'you'.*

Clearly, since Crick wrote about 'consciousness neurones', much
progress has been made in terms of the mapping of brain function.
We now know far more precisely which parts of the brain are
involved in thinking, monitoring sensations and controlling
activity. Nevertheless, with every advance in neuroscience, there
is the temptation to resort to his argument and suggest that we are
about to find the physical 'mind'. The logic of the argument does
not suggest that it is possible to do so. The firing of neurones in
my brain is one level of activity, thinking is quite another; the fact
that the latter depends on the former does not imply that the two
are identical.

Insight

In *Consciousness Explained* and other popular books on this
subject, Daniel Dennett, taking a materialist position, suggests
that, at some point in the future, a perfect neuroscience will
tell us all we need to know about the mind. My own view
is that it will tell us nothing more than we know now about
who we are as persons – it will simply show which neurones
fire when we think, experience or do various things.

AI AND NEURAL COMPUTING

To appreciate how the brain might be thought to create the mind,
one can look at two different areas of computer science:

▶ *Artificial intelligence (AI) uses computers to perform*
  some of the functions of the human brain. It works on
  the basis of knowledge and response, the computer stores
  memories and is programmed to respond to present
  situations which correspond to them. It can, for example,

recognize words, and can respond to them. The bigger the
computer memory, the more 'lifelike' this form of artificial
intelligence becomes.

▶ *Neural computing goes about its task quite differently.*
It tries to produce a computer which actually works like a
human brain – recognizing things, forming mental images,
even dreaming and feeling emotions. A neural computer,
although very simple by comparison, is like a brain in that it
programmes itself and learns from its environment.

Some scientists claim that AI holds the key. The human brain,
they argue, comprises about 100 million memories and a few
thousand functions. All you need, in a sense, is raw computing
power. On the other hand, this is never going to be that easy,
because attempting to match the human brain – the most complex
thing known in the universe – will take an enormous amount of
computer power.

This view is countered by those who claim that neural computing
holds the key to an understanding of the 'mind', since a neural
computer can take on characteristics that are normally regarded as
human. Human brains are not programmed, they just learn, and
that is also the defining feature of neural computing.

In other words

AI is the attempt to store and reproduce the workings of already
developed brains (of those who programme the computers); neural
computing is the attempt to get a simple artificial brain to 'grow' in
intelligence.

The difference between AI and neural computing highlights a
feature of Ryle's argument in *The Concept of Mind*. Ryle made the
distinction between 'knowing that' and 'knowing how'. He argued
that to do something intelligently is not just a matter of knowing
facts, but of applying them – to use information, not just to store
it. To do something skilfully implies an operation over and above
applying ready digested rules. To give one of Ryle's examples, a

clock keeps time, and is set to do so, but that does not make it intelligent. He speaks of the 'intellectualist legend', which is that a person who acts intelligently, first has to think of the various rules that apply to his or her action, and then think how to apply them (thus making 'knowing how' just part of 'knowing that' – knowing the rules for action as well as the facts upon which that action is based).

Ryle claims that when, for example, we make a joke, we do not actually know the rules by which something is said to be funny. We do not perform two actions, first thinking of the rules, and then trying to apply them. Rather, we simply say something that, in spite of not knowing why, actually strikes us as funny.

The same could be said for a work of art, literature or musical composition. The second-rate composer follows all the established rules and applies them diligently. He or she produces art that follows fashion. The really creative person does not follow rules, producing work that may be loathed or controversial, but nevertheless may be said to be an intelligent production, since it attempts to express something that goes beyond all previous experience or rules. This is a kind of 'knowing how': knowing how to perform creatively.

Now, if a computer is fed with sufficient information, it 'knows that'. It can also follow the process that Ryle calls the 'intellectualist legend' – it can sort out the rules and apply them to its new data. What it cannot do – unless we claim that it suddenly 'takes on a life of its own' – is to go beyond all the established (programmed) rules and do something utterly original.

By contrast, a neural network responds to each new experience by referring back to its memory of past experiences. In this way, it learns in the immediate context of its experience, not by predetermined rules. Everything is judged (by the neural network as well as by the human being) in terms of past experiences and responses, so that its understanding of the world is constantly changing. Its understanding is based on the relationships between events, not on rules.

Some philosophers, while accepting that the brain is the origin of consciousness, are suspicious of the computer-view of consciousness. John Searle of the University of California, Berkeley, believes that consciousness is part of the physical world, even though it is experienced as private and subjective. He suggests that the brain causes consciousness in the same sense that the stomach causes digestion. The mind does not stand outside the ordinary physical processes of the world. On the other hand, he does not accept that this issue will be solved by computer programs, and has called the computer-view of consciousness a 'pre-scientific superstition'.

While some hold that consciousness is really a higher order mental activity (thinking about thinking: being self-conscious) others claim that it is really a matter of the brain recognizing and relating the various sensations received by the body. So, for example, Professor Roger Penrose of Oxford (in *The Emperor's New Mind*, 1989) argued that it would be impossible to create an intelligent robot because consciousness requires self-awareness, and that is something that a computer cannot simulate. He argues that consciousness is based on a 'non-algorithmic' ingredient (in other words, an ingredient which does not depend on an algorithm – a set of rules).

For consideration

A robot would not need self-awareness in order to carry out actions intelligently, merely a set of goals to be achieved. So, for example, a chess program can play chess and beat its own creator, but it only knows what constitutes winning at chess, not the significance of playing the game.

Such discussions of artificial intelligence and neural networking take us well beyond the old mechanistic view of the universe, and therefore away from the kind of mind/body dualism that was introduced by Descartes. Intelligent activity is more likely to be seen now as a feature of complexity and of relationships. If something is complex enough, and if its operation is based on a constantly changing pattern of relationships between its memory components, then it appears to evolve in a personal and intelligent way; it takes on character.

Chinese writing

A most graphic way of exploring the difference between being able to handle and manipulate information (which a computer can do very efficiently) and actually understanding that information (which, it is claimed, a computer cannot) was given by the philosopher John Searle (in his 1984 Reith Lectures, *Minds, Brains and Science*):

You are locked in a room, into which are passed various bits of Chinese writing, none of which you can read. You are then given instructions (in English) about how to relate one piece of Chinese to another. The result is that you are apparently able to respond in Chinese to instructions given in Chinese (in the sense that you can post out of the room the appropriate Chinese reply), but without actually understanding one word of it. Searle argues that this is the case with computers; they can sort out bits of information, based on the instructions that they are given, but they cannot actually understand the information they are given.

The philosopher Hubert Dreyfus has given a criticism of AI based on an aspect of the philosophy of Heidegger (see p. 251). Heidegger (and Dreyfus) argued that human activity is a matter of skilful coping with situations, and this presupposes a 'background', which is all the facts about society and life in general that lead us to do what we do. Now AI, according to Dreyfus, attempts to reduce this 'background' to a set of facts ('know-how' is reduced to 'know-that'). But this is an impossible task, because there is an ever-growing number of facts to be taken into account; for practical purposes the number of background facts is infinite. Also, a person has to select which of those facts are relevant to the decision in hand, and the rules for deciding which are going to be relevant then form another set of facts that might also be infinite. It is therefore impossible to provide enough rules and facts to fill out the whole background to any human decision, and this is, according to Dreyfus (see Dreyfus and Dreyfus, *Mind over Machines*, 1986), a problem which will continue to be formidable for AI.

For reflection

It seems to me that artificial intelligence is basically a modern computerized form of Frankenstein's experiment! It is assembling 'materials' (in this case memory, processing power and the data upon which it is to work) in the hope that it will find the key to make this become a thinking being, a self. So far, the AI limbs have started to twitch, but the monster has not taken on human form!

and a comment ...

Over the last two decades, there has been a phenomenal rise in the power and sophistication of computers and in the way they are used, not least in connection with the internet, with its huge impact on commerce, communication and society. Much of what was written in this section appeared in the first edition of this book and reflected the situation in the mid 1990s. However, reviewing it fifteen years later, it seems that the fundamental issues concerning the relationship between computing and the human mind remain much the same, and those early arguments are still valid in our more computer-sophisticated environment.

Knowing me, knowing you

We now turn to some implications of the mind/body problem, particularly those that affect individuals in terms of their self-understanding, identity and knowledge of other people.

FREE WILL

Freedom of the will is a major feature in the mind/body debate. If, as a materialist or even a epiphenomenalist would claim, the mind is simply a by-product of brain activity, and if that brain activity, being part of a material world is, in theory, totally predictable, then there is no such thing as free will. We appear to be free only because we do not understand the unique combination of causes which force us to make our particular decisions. We are pawns of fate – if all causes were known, we would have no freedom and no responsibility for what we (erroneously) call our 'mental' operations.

In effect, the issue here is exactly the same as 'determinism' within the broader scope of the philosophy of science. We live in a world of cause and effect. If causality is universal (or if, as Kant, we believe that the mind automatically assumes that it is) then it provides a closed loop of explanation for everything that happens. Human beings and their choices, being part of the physical world, come within that loop.

Insight

There is a danger here of falling into a fallacy that the philosopher Henri Bergson called 'retrospective determinism'. Just because something has happened we are tempted to assume that it had to happen, and therefore search backwards for its necessary causes. This is not a sound argument for determinism, because it has already ruled out the possibility of genuine chance and spontaneous creativity before it starts.

Yet many people would want to argue that freedom and morality are an essential part of what it means to be a human individual. We are not robots, even sophisticated ones. Our role in the world is proactive, not reactive. We shape the world as much as we are shaped by it. From this perspective, it is difficult to see the mind as 'nothing more than' a by-product of brain activity.

Note

This topic is raised most often in discussions of ethics, since responsibility and blame imply freedom to choose how to act. Notice particularly how the branches of philosophy cannot remain in watertight compartments; our view of science will affect our philosophical psychology, and this in turn will have implications for both religion and ethics.

DISEMBODIED CONSCIOUSNESS

Clearly, it is only logical to believe that the mind or self can exist outside the body or survive the death of the body if you take a dualist view of the mind/body relationship – since if the mind is a product of, or inevitably bound up with the physical body (and particularly the brain), it could have no disembodied existence.

Quite apart from general religious beliefs about life beyond death, there is plenty of evidence for strange phenomena concerning the dead – such as the sighting of ghosts, or speaking with the dead at a séance – but such evidence is always open to interpretation, and a person who takes a strictly materialist standpoint will always find an explanation for the experience that does not stray towards the paranormal. Many would argue that a person who is recently bereaved or for whom the possibility of contacting the dead is highly charged emotionally, is hardly going to be able to give an objective and detached account. So while the evidence for life beyond death may be plentiful, it is unlikely to be objective or scientific.

Another form of disembodied consciousness concerns so-called 'out of body' experiences. These are generally associated with times of personal crisis or physical danger, while having an operation, for example. Some people have the sense that they have left their physical body 'down there' on the operating table, and are able to move away from it, observing what is happening to it as though watching from a distance.

About one in three people who come near to death in this way report a 'near-death experience', so it is not a rare phenomenon, nor is it limited to people of any particular set of religious or other beliefs.

An example

I was in a great deal of discomfort and pain. Suddenly, the sounds of the ward – the nurses bustling about, women laughing, the babies crying – all disappeared, and I just floated gently away from my bed, sideways at first, then up.

I know it sounds extraordinary, but I knew that I was dying. It was extraordinary, because all the pain and discomfort disappeared and I was conscious of light surrounding me, and I was warm – it was a beautiful feeling.

But then I thought of my mother, with whom I have a very strong bond, and I remember thinking that I can't do this to my mum. I made a conscious effort to return to my body, which I did – with a great jolt, as if I'd been thrown back. And immediately all the pain returned.

Sunday Telegraph, 30 January 1994, p. 11

Such experiences can be investigated to see if they can represent a genuine spatial removal from the physical body, or if they are simply a product of the imagination. If they were proved to be literally true, it would suggest that the mind/body relationship is dualistic, and that – even if related closely to what is happening in the brain – the mind cannot be simply identified with the brain. Others, however, would suggest that it is exactly the sort of oxygen starvation that the brain may suffer in approaching death that leads to these unusual experiences.

As in all cases where we try to evaluate the experience of individuals, a useful test is that which Hume applied to the accounts of miracles (see p. 176): Which is more likely, that the event actually happened as reported, or that the person reporting it is mistaken?

KNOWLEDGE OF OTHER MINDS

In a strictly dualistic view of bodies and minds, you cannot have direct knowledge of the minds of others. You can know their words, their actions, their writings, their facial and other body signals, but you cannot get access to their minds. For a dualist, knowledge of other minds therefore comes by analogy. I know what it is like to be me. I know that, when I speak, I am expressing something that I am thinking. Therefore, I assume that, when another person speaks, his or her words are similarly the product of mental activity.

From Ryle's point of view there is no problem. There is no 'ghost in the machine'; what we mean by 'mind' is the intelligent and communicative abilities of the other person. If I know his or her actions, words, etc., then I know his or her mind; the two things are one and the same.

Returning to an earlier question

What is the difference between an actor who is playing the part of a person in pain, and someone who is actually in pain?

If I say that the one *really* feels pain, while the other only appears to feel pain, do I not assume that there is some non-physical self which exists over and above the actual grimaces and moans that lead me to describe the person as being in pain?

But is it possible to know another mind directly? What about telepathy? Here we have the difficulty of knowing how to evaluate a phenomenon the validity of which may be challenged, and for which there is, at present, no scientific explanation. But actually, if we are considering what we understand by the self of mind, it makes little difference whether telepathy works between minds that are distinct from their respective bodies, or whether there is some as yet unexplained way in which brains manage to communicate with one another. So, in itself, it does not help us to decide between a materialist or a dualist position.

Of course, if what you are is not a fixed entity but a process – if you are your personal history of the things you have said and done – then knowing you is simply (although far from simple!) a matter of getting to know you by being with you, listening to what you say and the descriptions of your thoughts, watching your habitual responses to life, getting to anticipate your wishes.

Insight

This suggests that the self is not a hidden, unknowable entity, but the ongoing story of you as an individual, responding to your world, developing a pattern of values, interests and relationships that you can think about, describe and share with others.

In other words

Other minds can be known by:

▶ *observing bodies (e.g. Ryle)*
▶ *by analogy with myself (the dualist's position)*
▶ *by telepathy (if this is accepted as a proven phenomenon)*
▶ *because of the phenomenon of language (how could there be communication, unless there were minds with which to communicate?)*
▶ *by observing ongoing patterns of behaviour, relationships and stated wishes (getting to see what is important for that person, as a living intelligent being).*

Knowing oneself is rather different, in that we are immediately aware of our own thoughts, whereas the thoughts of others come to us via their words, gestures and appearance. This has led some people to argue that we can know only our own mind, and are therefore radically alone, surrounded by bodies in which we have to infer that there are other minds similar to our own.

Such a lonely view is termed **solipsism**, and this is the fate of those who think of the soul or mind as a crude, unknowable 'ghost', as caricatured by Ryle.

In practice, we actually get to know other people by observation, by considering what they say or write, and by judging how they deal with life. We can question them, in order to clarify their likes and dislikes, for example. But in the end, we still depend upon our own observation.

An example

I ask someone, whom I have invited to dinner that evening, if he likes strawberries. He replies that he does.

▶ If he is telling the truth, and I believe him, then I know at least one thing about his own private tastes.

▶ He could, however, be saying that he likes them in order to be polite (seeing that I am returning home with a punnet of strawberries in my hand when I ask him the question). I need to ask myself if, in my past experience of him, he is someone who is straightforward about his views, or if he is always anxious to please and agree with people. If the latter is the case, then I am really no nearer knowing if he really does like strawberries.

▶ I could observe him at the dinner table that evening. Does he savour the strawberries, or swallow them quickly? Does he appear to be enjoying himself, or does he suddenly turn rather pale and excuse himself from the table?

▶ Do I subsequently observe him buying and eating strawberries?

This is a simple example of weighing up the evidence for a person's private sensations. It would become far more complex if the question were, 'Did you have a happy childhood?' In this case, there are profound psychological reasons why the immediate response may not be the correct one. Indeed, such is the way in which the unconscious mind affects the conscious, that the person may not actually know if he was or was not happy. Moments of trauma may have been blocked off and unacknowledged. The whole process of psychotherapy is one of gradually unpicking the things that a person says, in the light of their actual behaviour and physical responses.

Knowledge of other minds is therefore a process of assessment, based on observation. It is not instantaneous (if it were, most therapists would starve!). It is constantly open for revision.

I meet up with a friend whom I have not seen for 20 years.

▶ *Do I now treat this senior executive as though he were still the scruffy 15-year-old I once knew, with unchanged tastes and habits? If so, we are unlikely to renew our friendship!*

▶ *I have to learn anew – check what remains of old views, check what has changed, ask about life's experiences and their impact.*

Notice the assumption that I make in all this: that I am getting to know another person as a communicating subject. I do not explore his brain, nor seek for any occult 'soul'. I simply recognize that he is a person who has views, feelings, thoughts, experiences, and that he can communicate them. That process of communication means that getting to know another person is a two-way process. It depends upon my observation and enquiries, but also upon the willingness of the other person to be known. Without the person's co-operation, even a very experienced psychotherapist would find it extremely difficult to get to know that individual's mind. You can build up a profile – he is this sort of person with those sort of interests – but you cannot get much of an idea of the person as a unique, rounded individual. Psychologists advising the police can suggest the sort of person who might have committed a particular crime, based on their experience of similar people, especially in the case of those with severe mental disturbance. But they cannot point to a particular individual.

Contrast this with knowledge of yourself:

▶ *It is instantaneous. As soon as I stop to reflect, I can say if I feel happy or not.*

▶ *It is based on sensation, not observation. I do not have to listen to my own words, or look at my facial expressions in a mirror in order to know if I am enjoying myself. I have immediate sensations of pleasure or pain.*

BUT:

▶ *It is not certain. Although my knowledge of myself is more reliable than the knowledge of anyone else, I may still be mistaken. If it were not so, we could never become confused about ourselves, for we would know and understand both our experiences and our responses to them. Adolescence would be negotiated smoothly, mid-life crises would never occur, psychotherapists and counsellors would become extinct. Alas, the process of knowing oneself is probably more complex than knowing another person.*

In knowing myself, I have two advantages over others:

1 *I have memory. This means that my own knowledge of events and my response to them is more immediate and detailed than the accounts given by others, although my memory may let me down, and (in the case of traumatic experiences) things may be repressed because they are too painful to remember. In such a case, for example of trauma in childhood, another person may have a clearer memory of what happened and of my response at the time than I have myself.*
2 *I can deliberately mislead others about my feelings and responses. Generally speaking, except for cases of strong unconscious motivation, I do not mislead myself.*

PERSONAL IDENTITY

There are many ways of identifying yourself:

▶ *son or daughter of –*
▶ *a member of a particular school, university, business*

- *a citizen of a country, member of a race*
- *an earthling (if you happen to be travelling through space, this might become a very relevant way of describing yourself).*

At various times, each of these will become more or less relevant for the purpose of self-identity. Relationships establish a sense of identity, and the closer the relationship, the more significant will be its influence on the sense of self. Aristotle held that friendships were essential for a sense of identity.

An example

Walking down a street in London, I am not likely to think of myself first and foremost as British (unless, of course, I am near a famous building, and am surrounded by foreign tourists). Yet if I travel to a far-flung and inaccessible part of the globe, I might well say, 'I'm British' as one of the first means of identifying myself.

- *In general, self-identification is made easier by emphasizing those things by which one differs from others around one at the time.*
- *Those who are fearful of having their individuality exposed tend to 'blend in' with a crowd, giving themselves an 'identity' in terms of shared values. In practice, this leads to group identity, not individual identity.*

In practice, identity is not a matter of body or mind only, but of an integrated functioning entity comprising both body and mind. Of course, once the process of analysis starts, it is difficult to find a 'self' that is not at the same time something else – but that is exactly the reason why identity is not a matter of analysis.

- **Analysis** *shows bits and pieces, none of which is 'you'.*
- **Synthesis** *shows the way in which body, mind and social function all come together in a unique combination – and that is 'you'.*

Identity is therefore a matter of synthesis, not of analysis. *You are the sum total, not the parts.*

Reflecting on location

▶ *Are your thoughts physically contained within your head, just because they originate in brain activity?*

▶ *Where are your friendships located? In your head? In the heads of your friends? Somewhere in space between the two? In a level of reality that does not depend on space, if there is such a thing?*

▶ *Think of a chat show on radio. The programme is put together by a team of people. It is broadcast across hundreds, perhaps thousands of miles. The words of the host spark off thoughts in the minds of thousands of listeners. Some respond and phone in to the programme. Where is this whole phenomenon of the chat show located? If it does not have a single physical location, what does that say about personal identity and personal communication? Can it be that our identity is not contained within a physical location, but is formed by networks of significance?*

Is it possible, in thinking about mind as the prime way of defining a self or person, to ignore the importance of physical identity? Consider therefore a world in which we were all physically identical:

▶ *You would not know if someone was young or old, male or female.*

▶ *You would not know if the person facing you were a relative, a friend, a stranger or an enemy.*

▶ *Other people would fail to recognize you, would have to ask who you are. Your name would probably mean nothing to them. You would be most unlikely to know if you had ever seen them before.*

How would society or relationships be able to develop in such a world? Physical differences are the starting point of recognition and shared experience. A world of clones is likely to be a world devoid of relationships.

More than once in this chapter we have turned to the idea of an actor, and the distinction between acting and reality. This is also relevant for an understanding of 'persons'. For example, Aldo Tassi, writing in *Philosophy Today* (Summer 1993), explored the idea of a persona (or mask) that an actor puts on. The actor projects a sense of self – the self who is the character in the play. In doing so, the actor withdraws his own identity. In the theatre, the actor can go off stage and revert to his own identity. In the real world, Tassi argues, we create a character in what we do, but we can never step outside the world to find another self 'off stage'. He refers back to Aristotle, for whom the soul is the substantial form of the body, but substance for Aristotle was not a static thing. The soul is not superadded to the body in order to make the body a living thing; rather, the body gets both its being and its life from the 'soul'. Tassi says: 'Consciously to be is to project a sense of oneself, that is to say, to "assume a mask".'

Insight

Personal identity, if Tassi is right, is dynamic rather than static; it is acted out and developed; it does not exist in terms of static analysis.

For reflection

Frankenstein's monster takes on character as the novel unfolds. It is not there in the inanimate materials from which he (or it) is fashioned. Do we ever achieve a definitive 'character' of our own? Can we maintain multi-personalities without moving in the direction of schizophrenia?

There is much that can be explored in terms of 'persons'. In recent philosophy this has been brought to attention by the work of

P. F. Strawson (1919–2006), a British philosopher known particularly for his work on the nature of identity, and for his exposition and development of the philosophy of Immanuel Kant. In 'Persons', an article first published in 1958, and 'Individuals', 1959, he argued that the concept of 'person' was prior to the popular analysis of it as an animated body, or an embodied mind. Rather, a person is such that both physical characteristics and states of consciousness can be ascribed to it. The concept of a 'person' has many practical and ethical implications:

▶ *In what sense, and at what point, can an unborn child be called a person?*
▶ *An unborn child has a brain, but cannot communicate directly. Is such communication necessary for it to be called a full human being? (Consider also the case of the severely handicapped. Does lack of communication detract from their being termed 'people'?)*
▶ *Does a baby have to be independent before being classified as a person? If so, do we cease to be human once we are rendered totally dependent on others, for example, on the operating table?*
▶ *What is the status of a person who goes into a coma?*

Insight

Morality depends on a sense of personal identity and therefore needs to take such issues into account.

MEMORY

Memories are personal, and they are also influential. You are what you are because you have learned from the past – and that learning depends on memory. A person who has lost his or her memory finds it difficult to function, is constantly surprised or bewildered by the response of others who claim long-established friendship or hatred. Our responses are determined by our memories.

Hume saw memories as a set of private images running through one's head. It follows that, if I say I have a memory of a particular thing, nobody else can contradict me, because nobody else has access to that particular bit of internal data. But what if one thinks that one remembers something and then is shown that it would not be possible, for example, that I remember the Second World War, only to find that I was born after it was over? I would have to admit that my memory was faulty, or perhaps that a war film had lodged such vivid images in my mind that I genuinely believed that I had lived through it. I remember the image clearly enough, and am not lying about it, but what I have forgotten is the origin of that image, the original experience (on film, in this case, rather than in reality).

Memory errors can sometimes be countered by the idea that the person imagined an event rather than remembered it. Again, there is no doubting the mental image, what is at doubt is the origin of that image.

Great feats of memory require sifting through the many facts and images that are habitually available to us, to more specific events: remembering a place leads to remembering a particular person who was seen there, which then leads on to remembering any suspicious actions that he or she may have made. The feature of such memory is that it is revealed bit by bit; something that was previously forgotten is now remembered because another memory has triggered it. Following serious crimes, an identically dressed person is sometimes sent to retrace the steps of the victim, hoping that it may trigger off a memory in a passer-by.

But just because we may have privileged access to our own memories, does not mean that we are infallible. Four people, giving accounts of the same dinner party, may all provide quite different versions of events. Our memories are selective, providing us with recall of those sense experiences which are deemed significant, and ignoring those that are not.

Memory also serves to develop the 'background' of our actions and thoughts (to use Heidegger's term). Faced with a choice in the present, my memory searches for similar experiences in the past, and the memory of them will influence the choice I now have to make. In this sense, memory is an ever-growing means of self-definition.

Cognitive science

Much of what we have been discussing in this chapter is related to the traditional mind/body problem, which developed out of the radical dualism of Descartes and the issues raised by it. By the latter part of the twentieth century, however, these problems (without necessarily being resolved) were set in a new and broader context which is generally known as cognitive science.

Cognitive science is an umbrella term for a number of disciplines which impinge upon ideas of the self or mind:

▶ *We have already considered the impact of computers on our understanding of mental process, and the development of Artificial Intelligence and neural networking.*
▶ *Neuroscience is now able to map out the functions of the brain, identifying areas that are associated with particular mental or sensory processes.*
▶ *Pharmacology is able to control behaviour by the use of drugs, bringing a whole new chemical element into our understanding of behaviour.*
▶ *There is an increased awareness of the influence of food additives and environment in influencing mental activity; how we feel may well reflect what we eat and drink.*

> *Clinical psychology looks at the way an individual's mind functions, taking into account both its conscious and unconscious workings.*

Clearly, there is no scope within this present book for examining all these disciplines. All we need to be aware of is the way in which science today is far more flexible in its approach to the mind than would have been the case a century or more ago.

Science needs data upon which to work. In the case of mental operations, one approach has been to examine the physical equivalent of the mental operation – generally in terms of brain function. Another has been to allow mental operations to provide their own physical data. For example, the behaviourist approach to gathering data was to set up experiments that involved actions and responses, and then measure those responses. Can this boxed rat learn – by rewarding it every time it does the right thing – to press a button in order to get food?

A key term here is **functionalism**. This approach sees mental operations as the way in which intelligent life sorts out how to react to the stimuli it receives. Let us take a crude example. If I put my hand on something hot, my body receives the sensation of burning. My mind then becomes aware of the pain, remembers that, if the hand is not removed from the heat, damage is likely to be done, and therefore decides that I should withdraw my hand. Muscles contract, the hand is withdrawn, and the pain subsides. We may not be able to tell exactly which neurones, firing in the brain, were responsible for each step in that operation. What we do know, however, is the mental functions that were performed. Mind is what mind does.

A functionalist reflection

I own several corkscrews. One is fairly straightforward; screw it into the cork, hold the bottle and pull upwards. Another, once

(Contd)

4. The philosophy of mind 131

screwed in, uses a lever function and is pulled from the side. The most sophisticated has arms that grip round the side of the bottle, and so on.

These are all corkscrews, not by virtue of how they operate, or what they look like, but simply by virtue of their function. Whatever gets a cork out for you is your corkscrew!

Does it make any difference if an action is performed by a computer or by a human brain? We may not appreciate the difference in the mechanics by which each performs the operation, but the function is the same. There is a gap (usually referred to as the 'Leibniz' gap') in our knowledge, because we cannot see the point at which the physical and the mental interact. But does that matter, provided that we understand how the mental and physical function together?

Hence, a functionalist is able to produce what amounts to a map of the mind; a map that shows the different functions that the mind performs. What it cannot do, and argues that it is not necessary to do, is to wait to find out what each physical or electrical component does in the chain of events, before the significance of the mental function can be appreciated.

INTENTIONALITY

The idea of intentionality predates cognitive science, but is relevant to the broad range of issues that it considers. It originated in the work of the nineteenth-century psychologist Franz Brentano (1838–1917) and influenced the philosopher and psychologist William James (1842–1910). Intentionality, put simply, is the recognition that every perception and every experience is directed towards something. I do not just experience the shape of an apple before me, but I experience it as something to eat. In other words, mental functions shape and interpret what we experience – and we cannot have experience except as experience 'of' something.

Experience is about living in the world, relating to it, getting what we need from it, influencing it. It is not a separate and detached play of passing sense data. The mind takes an 'intentional stance' towards what it experiences.

Linking ideas

One may trace lines of thought from intentionality, through functionalism and (via William James) pragmatism, and even – as far as language is concerned – through the later developments of Wittgenstein's thought. We are not passive observers of the world. That is not why we have developed sense organs and brains. We have senses and minds in order to function, to find tools around us by which we can survive in a hostile environment or enjoy a comfortable one. Mind and thought is about relating and doing; when we observe, we do so with intentionality; our senses are judged by the function they perform in our life; and we take a pragmatic view of their operations. Wittgenstein said that, in order to understand it, one should look at how language is used, what function it plays in life. The same could be said of mind: intentionality, functionalism and pragmatism all suggest that we will only understand mind by considering what it does, not by standing back and trying to analyze what it is.

A 'personal' postscript

The mind/body issue, perhaps more than any other, illustrates the problem of the analytic and reductionist approach to complex entities. Frankenstein got it wrong! The analysis and reassembling of the components of a human being, whether it be a crude autopsy to hunt for the elusive 'soul', or the sophisticated attempt to reproduce the process of thinking with the aid of computers, is, I am convinced, unlikely to produce more than a caricature of a human person.

The experience of being a thinking, feeling and reflecting person is not susceptible to analysis, because it is not *part of* the world we experience. Wittgenstein was right in saying that the self was the limit of the world, rather than part of it.

Nor is the self a fixed entity. Hume could never see his mind except in the procession of thoughts that passed through it. From birth to death, there is constant change, and our thoughts of today shape what we will be tomorrow.

Insight

Throughout life, we leave our imprint on the world around us: words we speak, actions we perform, roles we assume. It is these that form our changing story, and define our character from moment to moment.

Even our process of reflection, the most private of activities, is dependent upon the outside world. It is extremely difficult to experience something with absolute simplicity or purity, for we immediately categorize it and understand it 'as' something. We cannot help doing that, because the way we think is shaped by our common language, common culture and the whole range of ideas and experiences that we share with others. As soon as we explain ourselves, we are engaged in a social activity; private language is meaningless.

Philosophers and scientists tend to think – that is their job, but it is also their problem! They search around in the mental jungle for ideas, concepts, theories and evidence. Hence they find it difficult to locate the self or explain its nature, for they launch into an analysis, using the product of mind in order to try to define the nature of mind itself. They focus in upon that which focuses in upon itself focusing in upon itself, and so on. In the spiral of analysis, the self becomes elusive and vanishes.

By contrast, those who *meditate*, who still the mind until it is gently focused on a single point, become aware of something very different. The self becomes empty, becomes nothing and everything at the same moment. There is no separate 'self' waiting to be discovered, only an ongoing process of thinking, experiencing and responding. Returning to the world of everyday experience, however, the 'self', as we conventionally understand it, continues its ever-changing patterns of thought, feeling and response. Without some idea of self we could not function nor relate to others; we may not know exactly what it is, but we know we cannot make sense of people and relationships without it.

Insight

The mind (as a separate, definable thing) is a convenient illusion, a shorthand term we use for the ongoing personal process of experiencing, thinking and responding that is our life as an intelligent being.

10 THINGS TO REMEMBER

1 *Materialism generally identifies the mind with (and restricts it to) activity in the brain.*

2 *Dualism sees the mind as non-physical, but has problems showing how it interacts with the body.*

3 *The idea of life beyond death depends on a dualist view of the mind.*

4 *Computers replicate brain function but not the experience of consciousness.*

5 *Knowledge of other minds is problematic for a dualist.*

6 *We define ourselves by ways in which we differ from others.*

7 *The experience of personal identity depends on memory.*

8 *Neuroscience shows how specific brain activity relates to elements of thought and experience.*

9 *'Functionalism' is the term for studying what the mind does, rather than what it is.*

10 *The self is a process, rather than a fixed entity.*

5

The philosophy of religion

In this chapter you will learn:
- *about religious experience and how it may be described*
- *about the arguments for the existence of God*
- *about miracles, the problem of evil and other key issues.*

In Western thought, the philosophy of religion is concerned with:

▶ *Religious language: what it means, what it does and whether it can be shown to be true or false.*
▶ *Metaphysical claims (e.g. that God exists): the nature of the arguments by which such claims are defended, and the basis upon which those claims can be shown to be true or false.*

In addition to these basic areas of study, there are many other questions concerning religious beliefs and practices which philosophy can examine:

▶ *What is faith? How does it relate to reason? Is it ever reasonable to be a religious 'fundamentalist'?*
▶ *What is 'religious experience' and what sort of knowledge can it yield?*
▶ *Is the universe such as to suggest that it has an intelligent creator and designer?*

- *Are miracles possible? If so, could we ever have sufficient evidence to prove that?*
- *Is belief in a loving God compatible with the existence of suffering and evil in the world?*
- *Can psychology explain the phenomenon of religion?*
- *Is life after death possible? If so, what difference does it make to our view of life?*

Faith, reason and belief

Is religious belief based on reason? If it were, it would be open to change, if the logic of an argument went against it. However, experience tells us that most religious people hold beliefs that, while they may be open to reasonable scrutiny, depend on a prior commitment or wish to believe, and therefore belief may persist in the face of reasonable criticism.

Within Christianity, there is a tradition – associated particularly with the Protestant Reformation and Calvin – that human nature is fallen and sinful, and that human reason is equally limited and unable to yield knowledge of God. Belief in God is therefore a matter of faith, and any logical arguments to back that belief are secondary.

Note

The last sentence speaks of belief 'in God' and not just belief 'that God exists'. That is a crucial difference, and we shall return to it on p. 171. Belief 'in' something implies an added element of commitment and valuation. One might, after all, believe 'that' God exists, but think that such belief is quite trivial and of no personal significance, which is not what believing 'in' something is about.

Insight

Hence the frustration of some debates between atheists and believers. The one expects that reason and evidence will settle the matter; the other has deep emotional and intuitive 'reasons' for believing. But the key question is: can you believe 'in' something, if you do not also have reasons to believe 'that' it exists? Is spiritual intuition alone enough?

The quest for certainty is sometimes termed **foundationalism** – the attempt to find statements that are so obviously true that they cannot be challenged. We have already seen that Descartes came to his incontrovertible statement 'I think, therefore I am.' Some modern philosophers of religion, notably Alvin Plantinga, argue for a 'Reformed Epistemology'. That is, a theory of knowledge that, like the theologians of the Reformation, is based on basic beliefs that are self-evident to the person who holds them, even if they are not open to reasoned argument. An example of this would be the belief that the universe is designed by God, based on a sense of wonder and beauty. We shall look at the 'design argument' on p. 163; what is different here is that Plantinga thinks that such belief is not a logical conclusion to an argument, but is held *prior to* engaging with that argument.

A related idea is **fundamentalism**. Originally used as a term for those who wished to set aside the superficialities of religion and return to its fundamental principles, it is now more commonly used for those who take beliefs, as they are found in the Bible or the Qur'an for example, in a very literal and straightforward sense and apply them without allowing them to be challenged by reason. A basic problem with this is that the scriptures were written using particular language and in a particular context, and if statements are taken literally and out of context, the original intention of the writers may be lost. Of course, the fundamentalist would not accept this, believing that the words of scripture are given directly by God and are therefore not open to any form of literary or contextual analysis.

That something more than logic is needed if we are to understand the nature of religious statements was highlighted by the Danish philosopher Søren Kierkegaard (1813–55). He argued that a 'leap of faith' was necessary, and that it was not so much the content of a belief that made it religious, but the way in which it is believed – with subjectivity and inwardness.

PASCAL'S WAGER

Blaise Pascal (1623–62) put forward what must count as one of the saddest pieces of logic ever employed within the philosophy of religion. His *Pensées* were published posthumously in 1670. In them, Pascal battles (as did his contemporary Descartes) with the implications of **scepticism** – the systematic challenging of the ability to know anything for certain. Pascal was a committed Catholic and wanted to produce an argument that would both justify and commend belief.

To appreciate the force of his argument, you need to be aware that his view of human nature was rather bleak: without God's help, people were inherently selfish, and would only do what seemed to be in their own self-interest. He also believed that non-believers would see the life of religion as one which would limit their freedom, and would therefore appear to go against their self-interest. His famous 'wager' is an attempt to counter this view.

His starting point is that reason alone cannot prove that God exists; to believe or not believe therefore involves an element of choice. Which choice is in line with enlightened self-interest, and therefore likely to appeal to the non-believer? His argument runs like this:

- ▶ IF *I believe in God and he does indeed exist, I stand to gain eternal blessings and life with God after my death.*
- ▶ IF *I believe in God and he does not exist, all I lose is any inconvenience of having followed the religious life – inconvenience that he considers negligible.*